Highlights

Make Your Own
Comic
Adventures

KID TESTED BY
LILLYAN
BORGER,
AGE 10

HIGHLIGHTS PRESS
Honesdale, Pennsylvania

WHAT'S INSIDE

Learn to draw monsters like me!

MONSTERS

Finish the Comic.................................8–9
Monster Doodles 10–11
Roaring Jokes 12
Sticker Story 13
Ghastly Word Search 14
Just Sayin' 15
Draw a Monster..............................16
Comic Creator 17

SUPERHEROES

Finish the Comic..............................20–21
Sticker Sound Effects 22–23
Just Sayin'.....................................24
Superpower Quiz 25
Superhero Doodles 26–27
Super Word Search 28
Hidden Pictures.............................29
Draw a Supermobile.......................30
Comic Creator 31

What's my superpower?

YOU'LL *NEVER* GUESS WHAT I HAD FOR DINNER.

ANIMALS

Finish the Comic..............................34–35
Animal Doodles..............................36–37
Funny Fill-In 38
Animal Mix-Up 39
Creature Code 40
Just Sayin'.....................................41
Draw a Grumpy Bear......................42
Comic Creator 43

Are you yeti to find me?

MYTHICAL CREATURES

Finish the Comic............................46–47
Mythical Doodles 48–49
Just Sayin'....................................50
Creature Creation..........................51
Mythical Criss-Cross 52
Bigfoot's Coming!..........................53
Draw a Unicorn.............................54
Comic Creator...............................55

SPACE

I promise I won't byte.

A-maze-ing Space Mission 58–59
Space Doodles 60–61
Geared-Up Maze............................62
Just Sayin' 63
Draw a Robot 64
Build a Bot..................................65
Just Sayin'...................................66
Space Code 67
Draw an Alien 68
Comic Creator 69

Never miss a clue!

IT'S A MYSTERY

Finish the Comic............................72–73
Detective Doodles 74–75
Scene of the Rhyme 76–77
Find the Spies...............................78–79
Just Sayin'....................................80
What's Your Disguise? 81
Draw Spy Gear 82
Comic Creator...............................83

EXTRA ADVENTURES

Face Time!....................................4–5
The Comic Pages 6–7,
                    18–19, 32–33, 44–45,
                    56–57, 70–71
Scrambled Sounds 84
Caption This!................................85
Comic Creator...............................86–92

Answers 93–96

Use your stickers to make your adventures POP!

FACE TIME!

Draw faces on these characters, then draw some of your own!

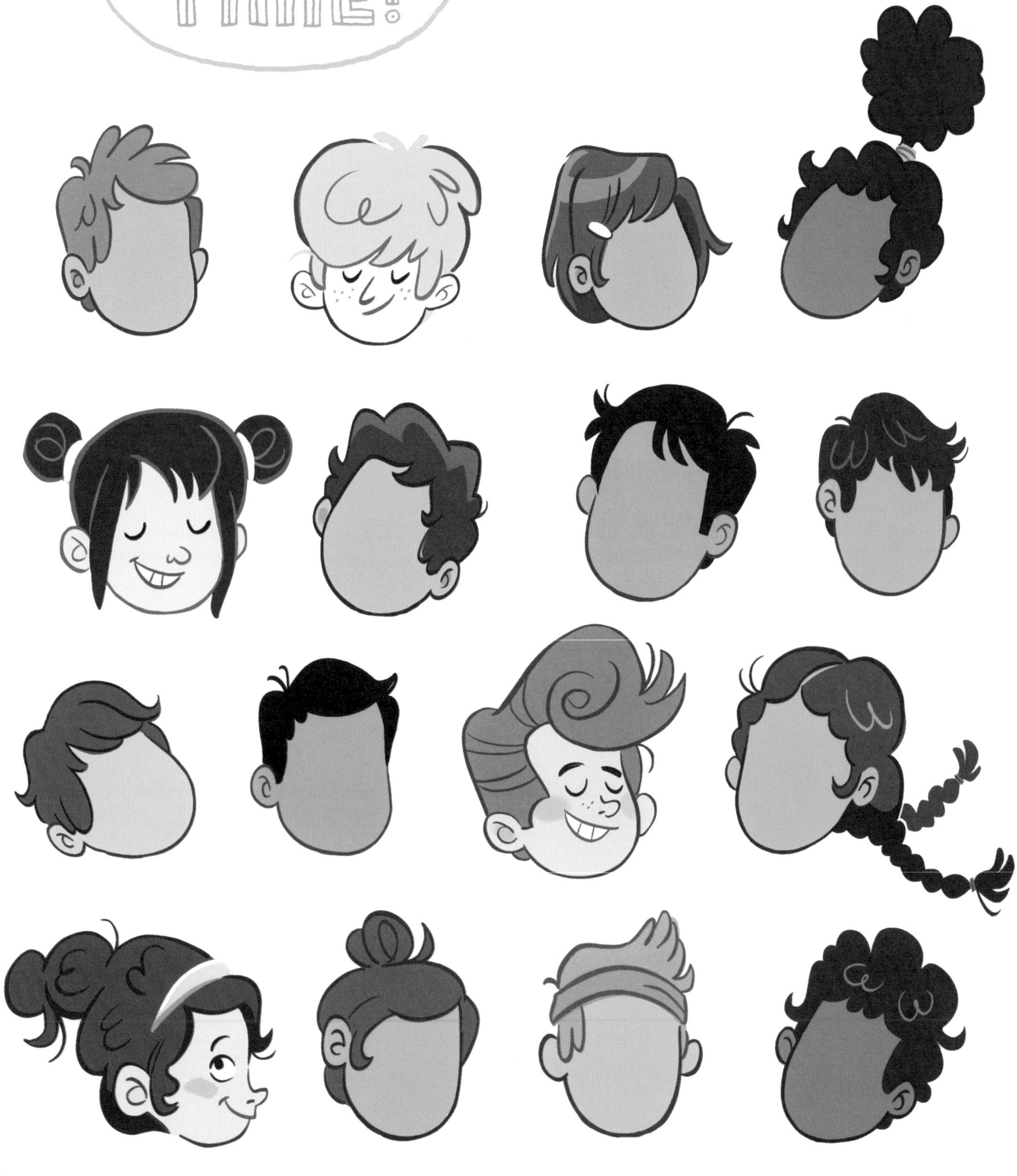

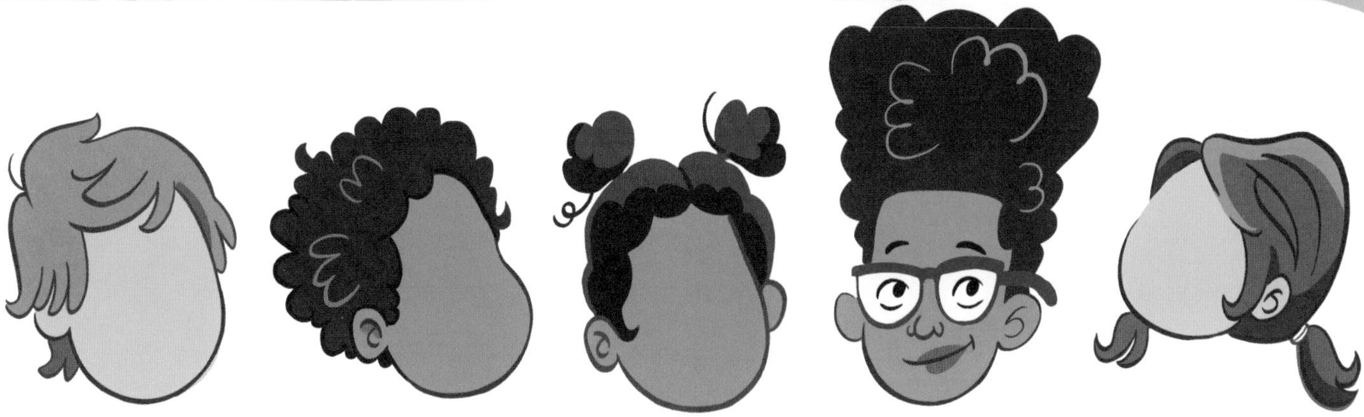

KEEP CARTOONING!

Copy your favorite features and expressions from this book and other comic books to practice drawing more faces.

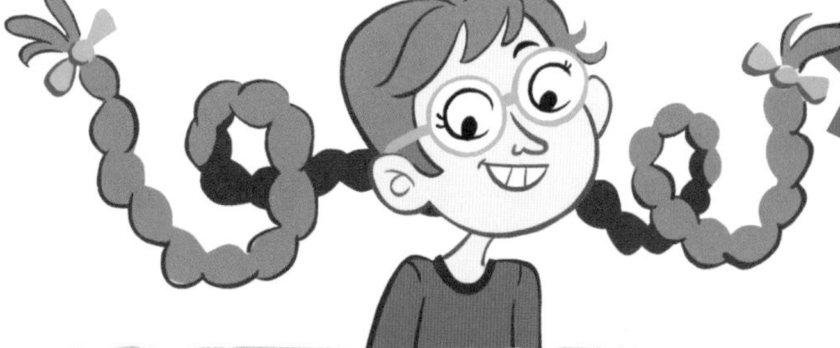

THE COMIC PAGES

The speech balloons are missing in these cartoons. Can you figure out which sticker belongs with which cartoon?

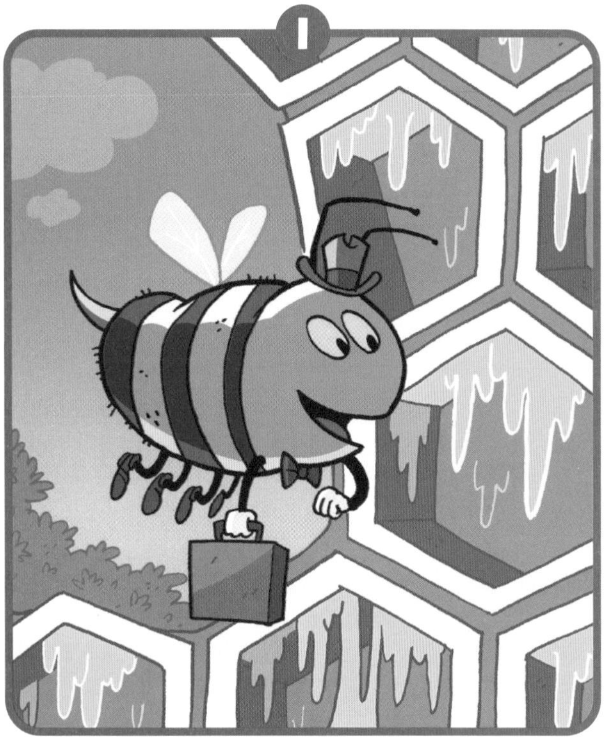
1

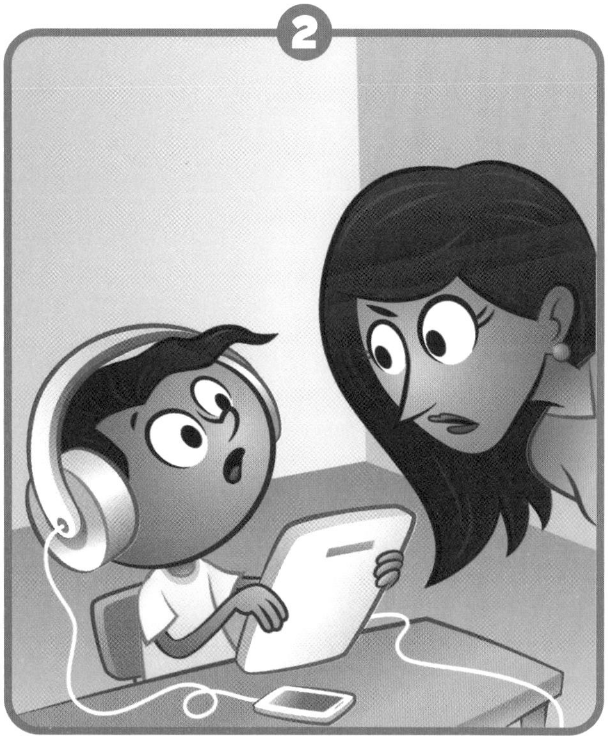
2

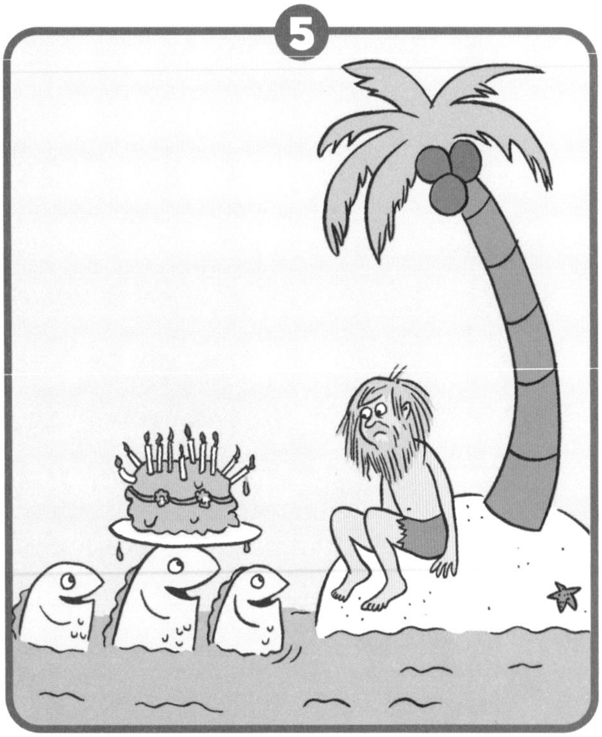
5

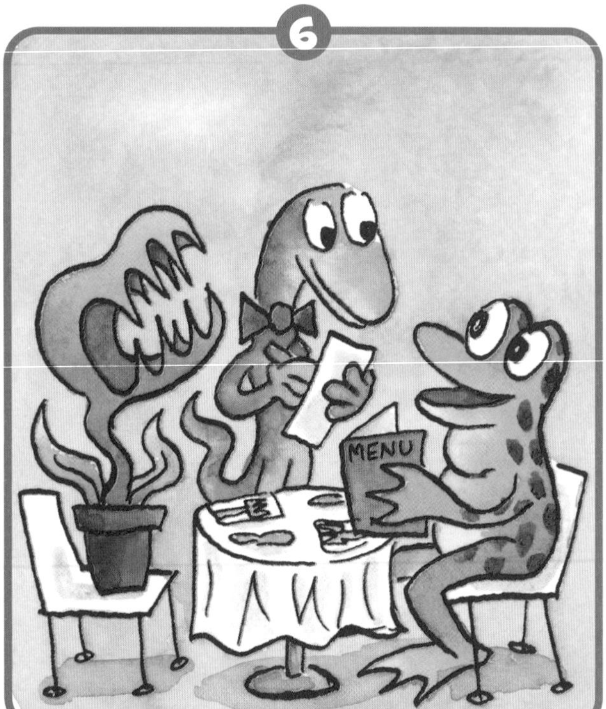
6
MENU

3

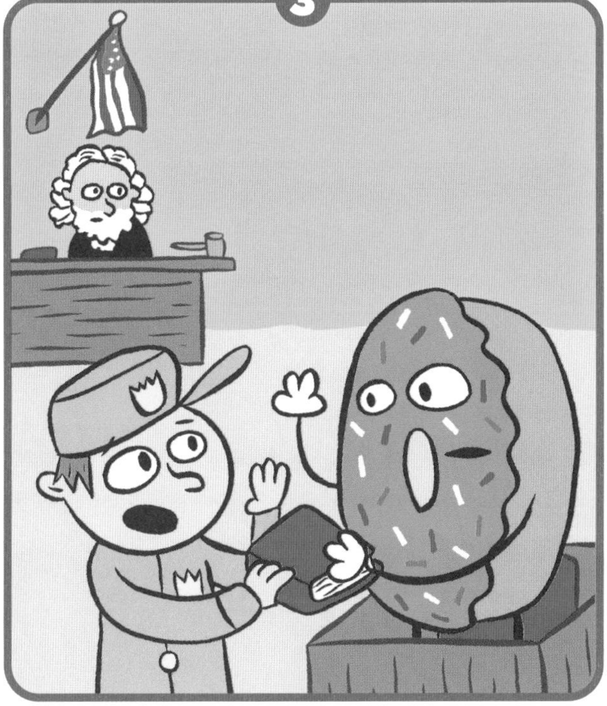

4

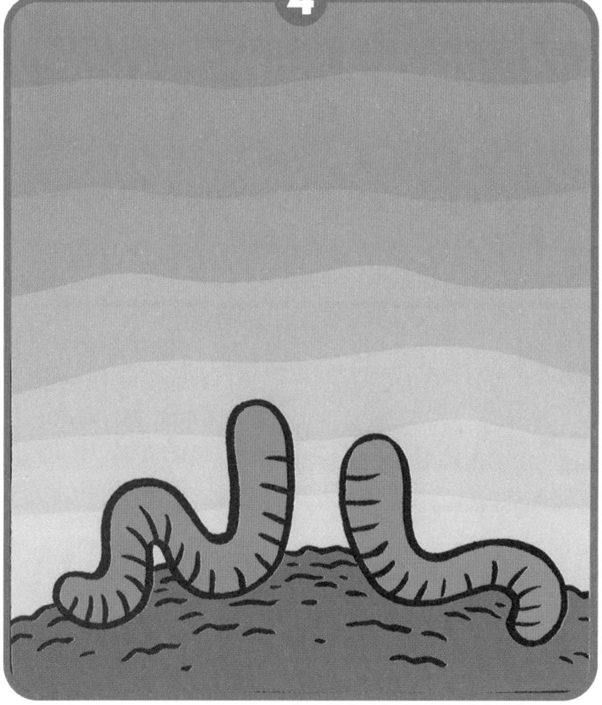

7

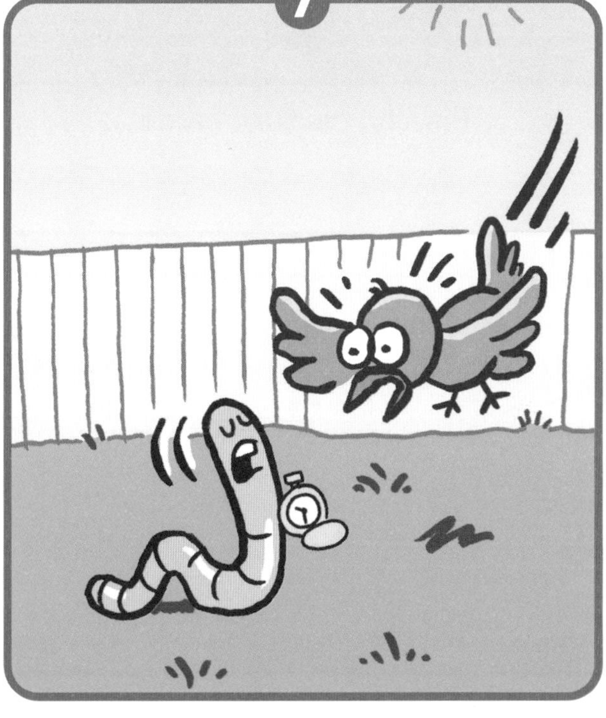

8

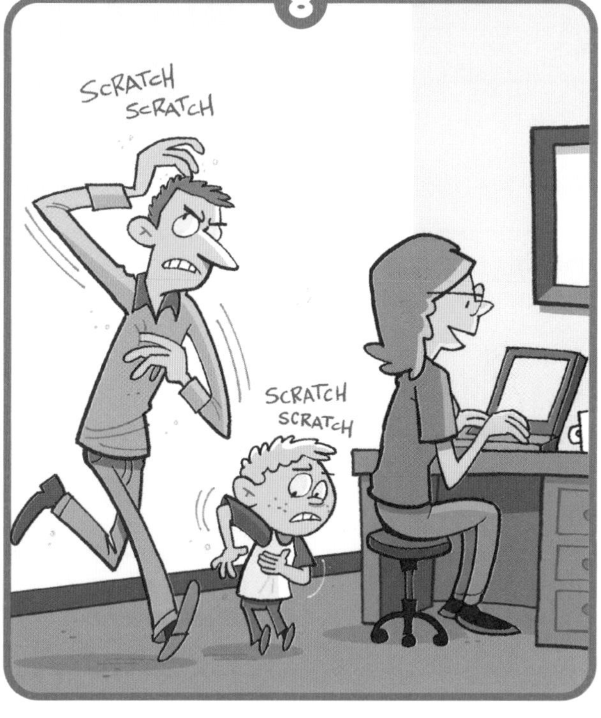
SCRATCH
SCRATCH
SCRATCH
SCRATCH

Finish the Comic

Odo's Perfect Job

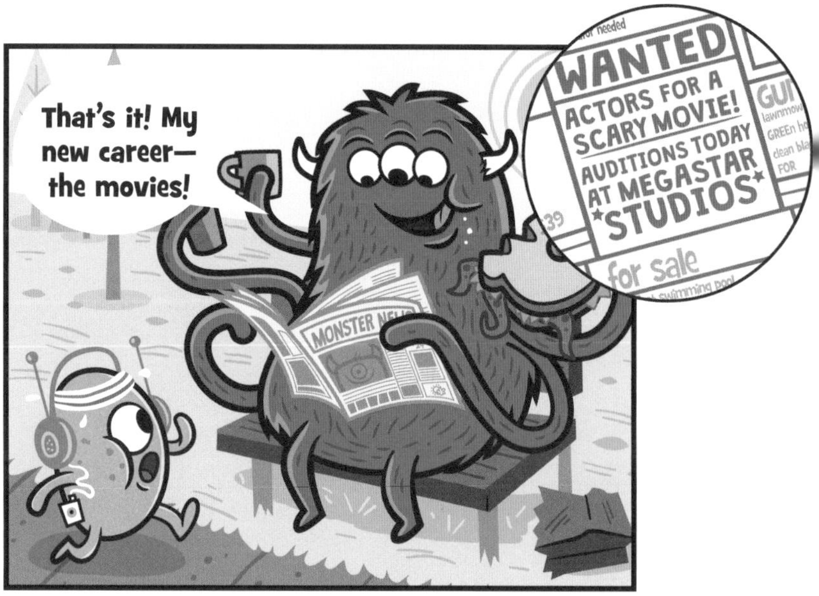

That's it! My new career—the movies!
WANTED
ACTORS FOR A SCARY MOVIE!
AUDITIONS TODAY AT MEGASTAR STUDIOS
for sale

While Odo ate his lunch in the park, he read job ads.

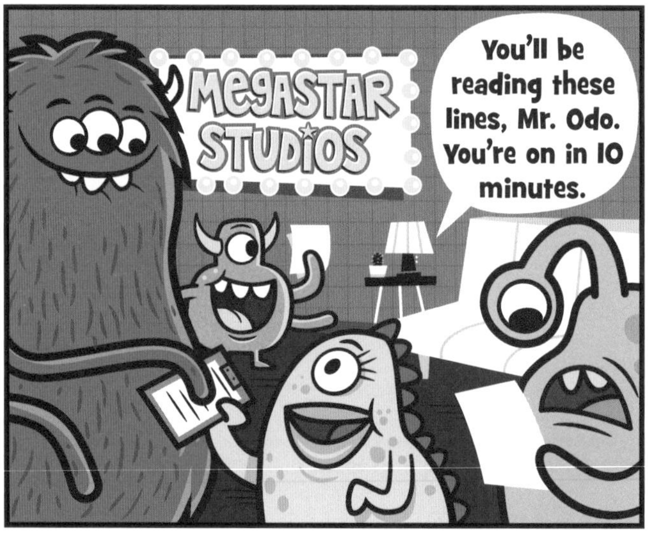

MEGASTAR STUDIOS
You'll be reading these lines, Mr. Odo. You're on in 10 minutes.

He rushed over to Megastar Studios. The waiting room was crowded.

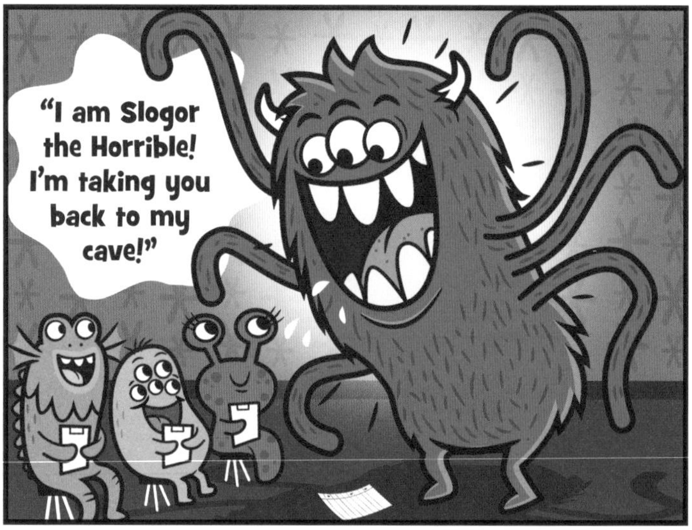

"I am Slogor the Horrible! I'm taking you back to my cave!"

Finally, his turn came.

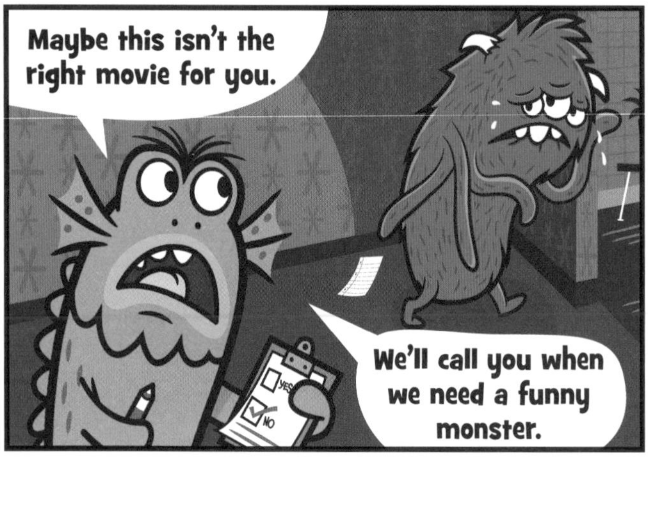

Maybe this isn't the right movie for you.
We'll call you when we need a funny monster.
YES
NO

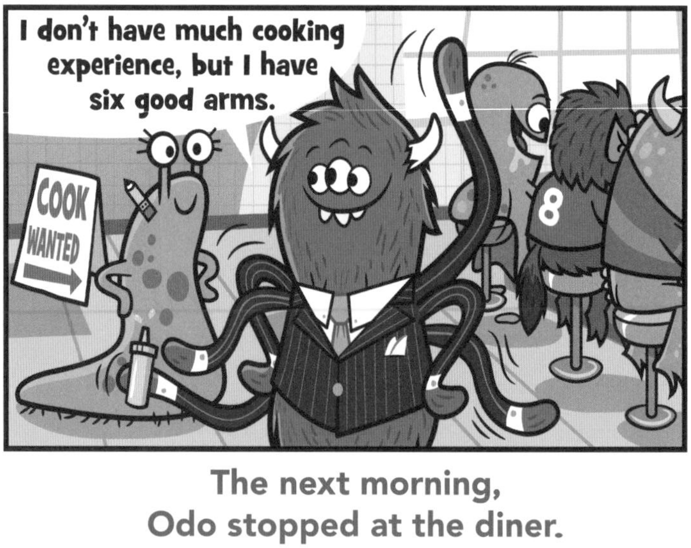

I don't have much cooking experience, but I have six good arms.
COOK WANTED

The next morning, Odo stopped at the diner.

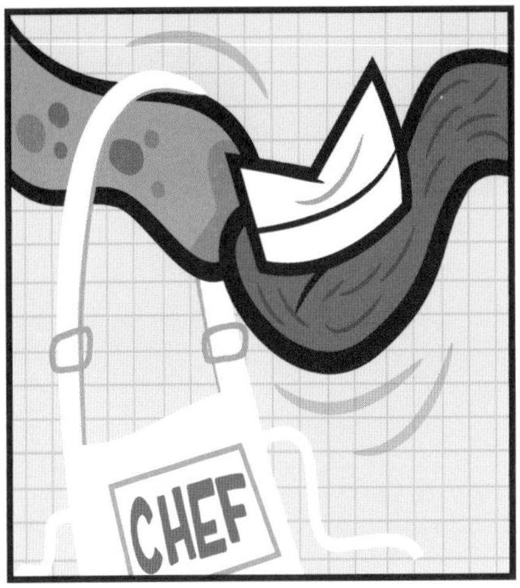
CHEF

"Well, I do need help with the morning rush."

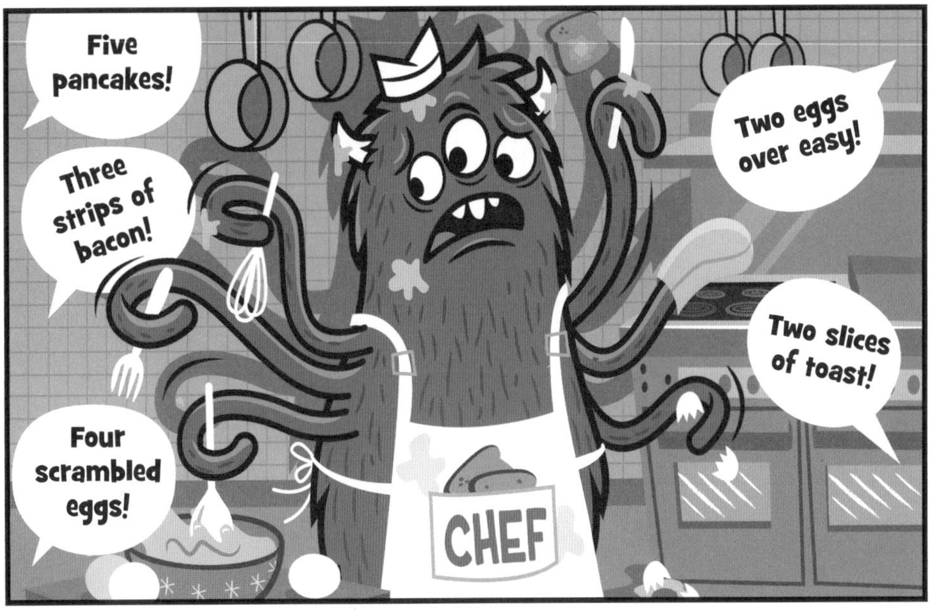
Five pancakes!
Three strips of bacon!
Four scrambled eggs!
Two eggs over easy!
Two slices of toast!
CHEF

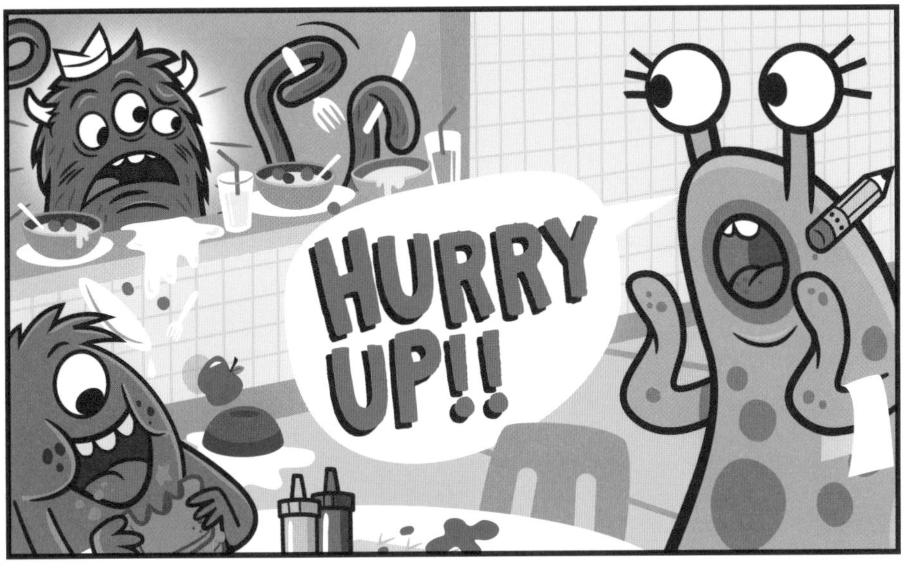
HURRY UP!!

Odo tried to keep up, but the orders came too fast.

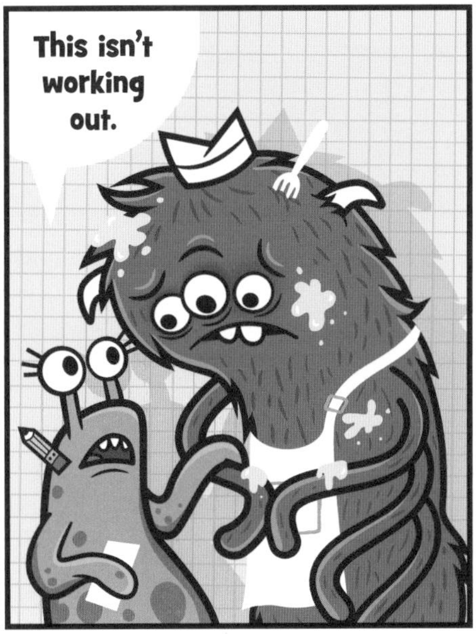
This isn't working out.

Finally, Odo realized what his job should be.

What job should Odo have? Draw what you think it is here.

MONSTER DOODLES

There are lots of ways to draw a monster. Finish drawing these monsters, then try drawing all the monsters you can think of. Don't forget to use your stickers!

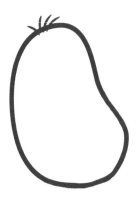

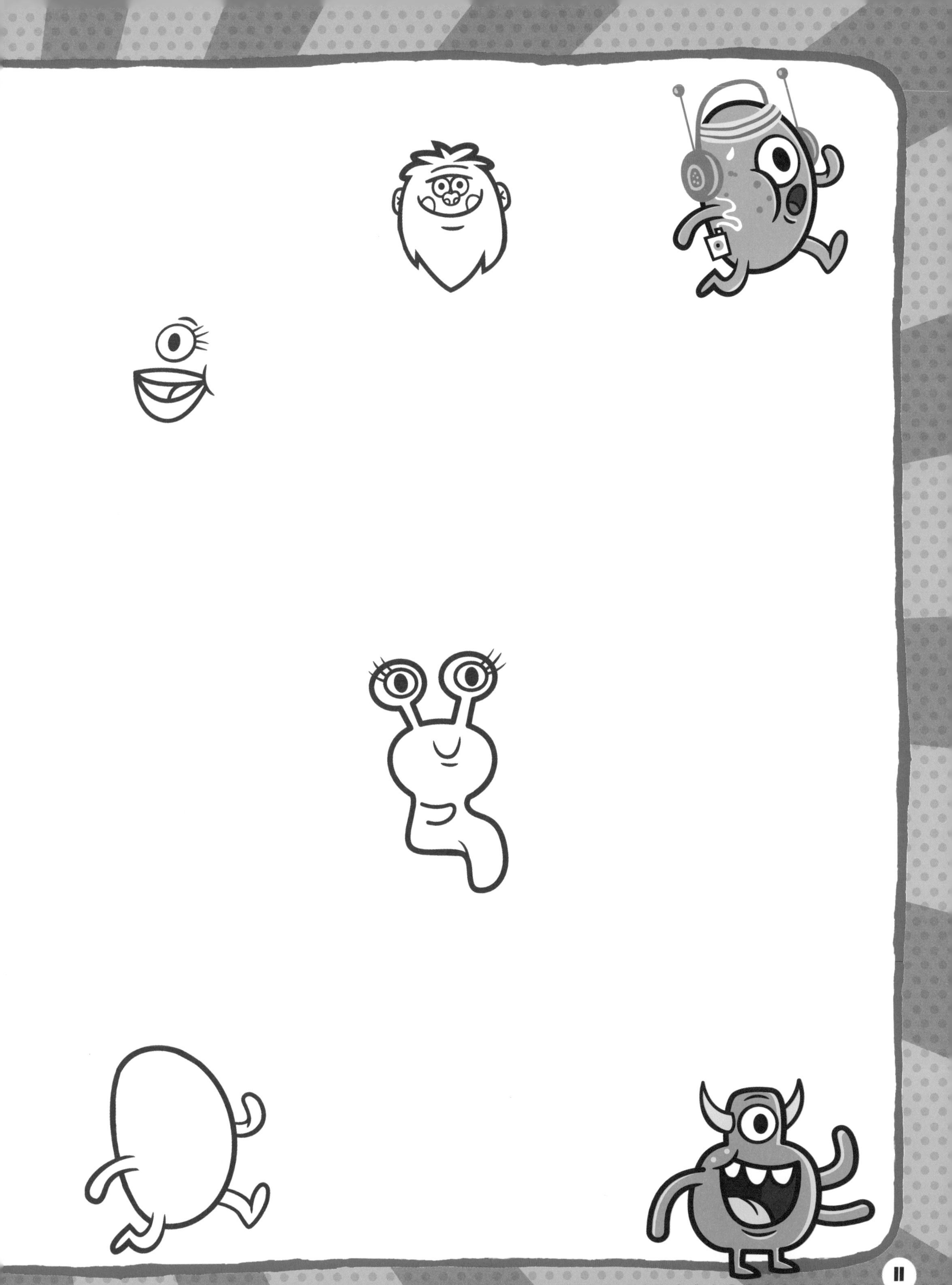

ROARING JOKES

Use the monster names to solve the codes. We did the first one for you. Each coded space has two numbers. The first number (6) tells you which monster name to use. The second number (1) tells you which letter in that monster's name to use. Fill in the rest to answer these monster jokes!

Monster List

1. GODZILLA
2. SASQUATCH
3. BASILISK
4. GOBLIN
5. ZOMBIE
6. LOCH NESS
7. WEREWOLF
8. BIGFOOT
9. BOGEYMAN
10. VAMPIRE

Where do monsters go to water ski?

L ___ ___ ___   ___ ___ ___ ___ ___

6-1 9-7 3-8 9-4   5-6 7-4 10-6 1-5 6-6

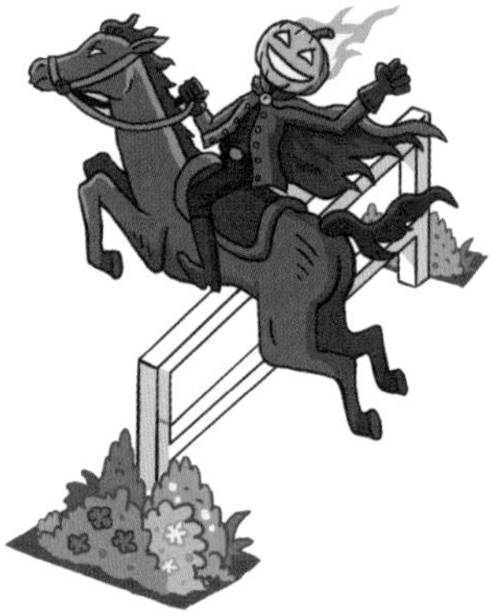

What do you call a giant mummy?

___ ___ ___ ___ ___ ___ ___ ___

4-1 10-2 2-5 1-4 5-5 7-7 3-5 2-2

What is a ghost's favorite party game?

___ ___ ___ ___ - ___ ___ ___ - ___ ___ - ___ ___ ___ ___ ___ ___

6-4 8-2 1-3 10-7 - 10-2 9-8 1-3 - 4-1 6-2 - 6-7 2-9 7-3 10-5 5-6 3-8

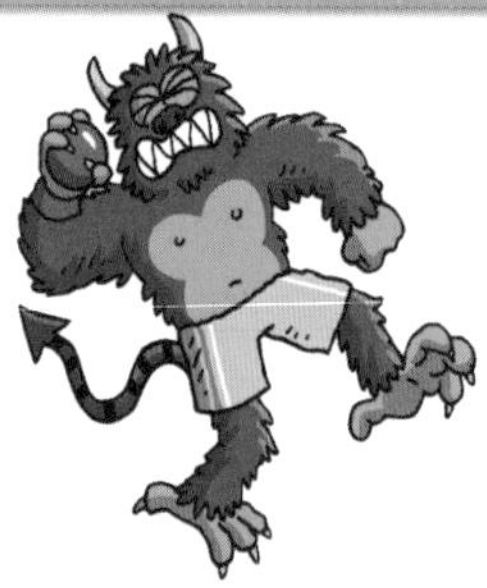

What do monsters put on for sunny days?

___ ___ ___ ___ ___ ___ ___ ___ ___

3-3 2-5 4-6 6-7 2-8 7-3 9-4 10-2 5-3

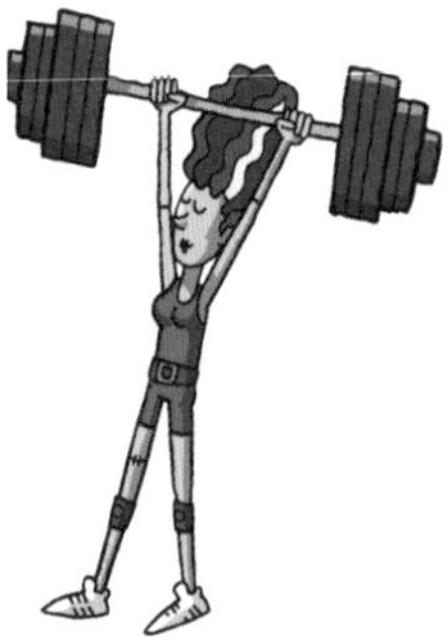

What is a ghost's favorite day?

___ ___ ___ ___ ___ ___ ___ ___ ___

8-4 7-3 3-6 4-1 6-4 2-7 1-3 10-2 9-5

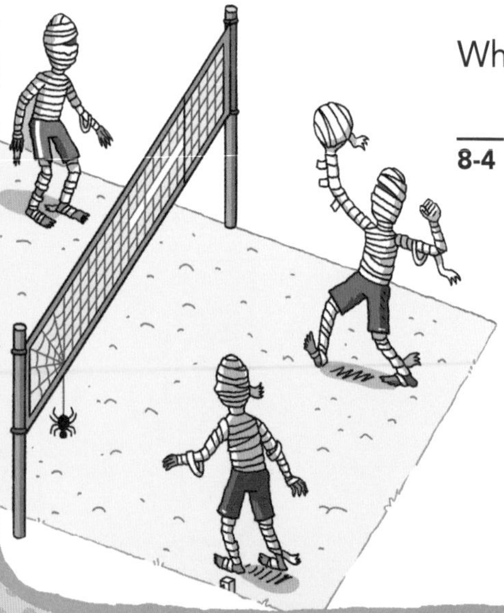

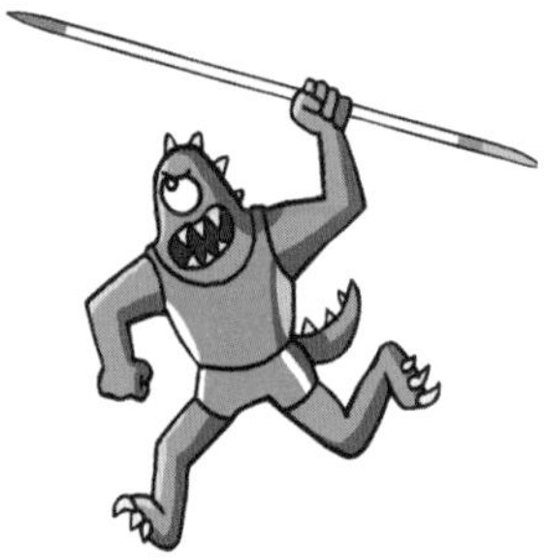

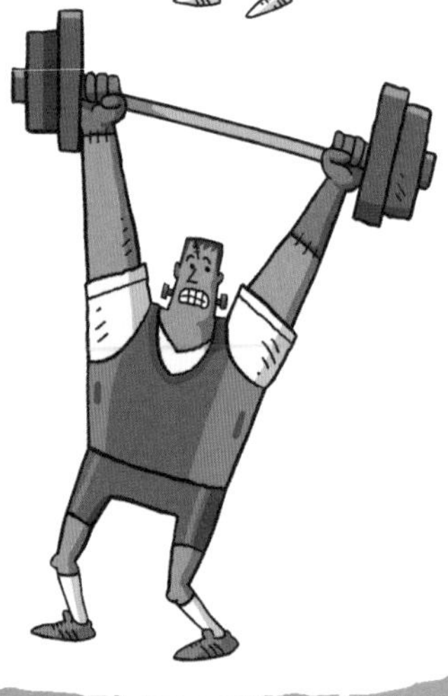

STICKER STORY

This just in! These breaking-news updates are making headlines. But something's giving the network team technical difficulties. Fill in the missing parts of the headlines by using your stickers to keep the news rolling!

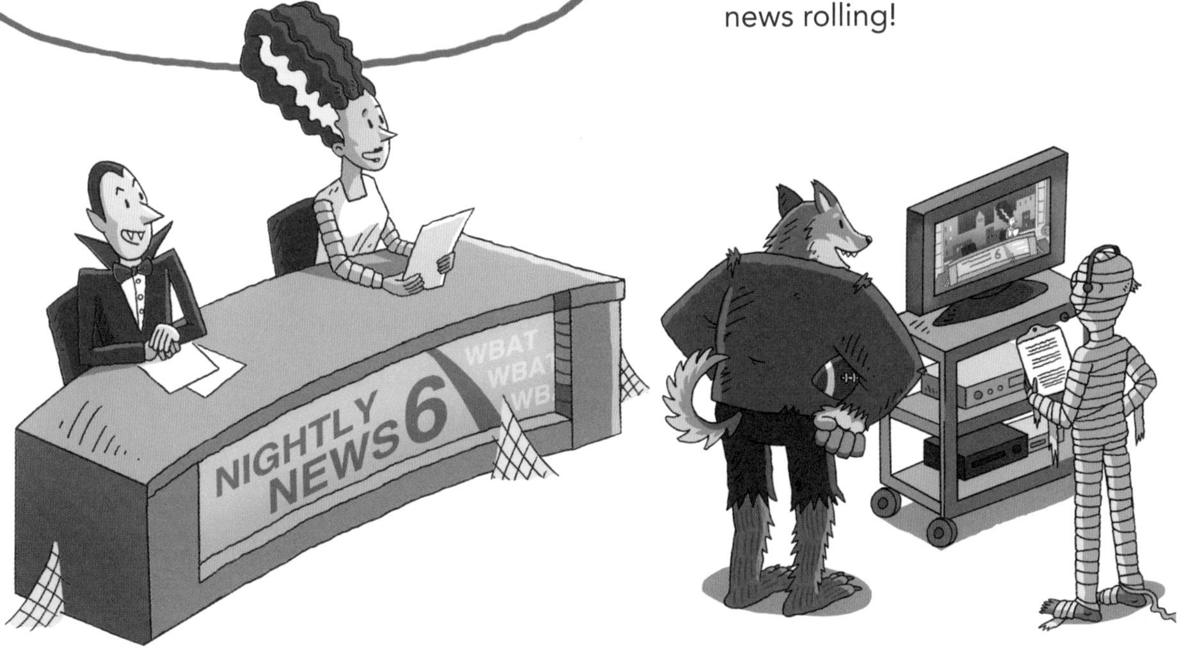
NIGHTLY NEWS 6
WBAT

Live: Coffin News Network

FURRY __________ FLYING AROUND __________ CAUSE SPECULATION

STUDY FINDS THERE ARE MORE __________ IN THE __________ THAN ONE MIGHT THINK!

DECISION TO REMOVE NOISY __________ CHANGES HOW __________ COMMUTE TO SCHOOL

ADVICE FROM __________ ON CHANNELING OUR INNER __________

RECENT TREND IN __________ CAUSES __________ TO LOOK PALER THAN EVER BEFORE

CONFUSED __________ DISCOVERED AFTER __________ VISIT

GHASTLY WORD SEARCH

There are 21 monsters hidden in this grid. Look for them up, down, across, backward, and diagonally. Find them all and you'll be a monster master!

```
N I E T S N E K N A R F L
M I N O T A U R N F R Z O
R E D Z R L L I K D O G C
Y E D U J A U L A N B Y H
E Z P A S C M U S M B R N
T E Q A M O W I Z A R W E
I L I M E E K Y K I W O S
T B J B T R M E P M M L S
S A I D M O A V M L T F M
O C O G F N V Z L W G M O
H T J W E O J J R G L A N
G S O K J O I I K L N Y S
I L Y B O I Y K J Y E G T
F M U M M Y D T K H N O E
S P O L C Y C C U H Y B R
Z M O C O M R H Y D E O C
```

Word List

BIGFOOT
BOGEYMAN
CYCLOPS
DRACULA
DR. JEKYLL

MR. HYDE
FRANKENSTEIN
GHOST
GODZILLA
GRIM REAPER

LOCH NESS MONSTER
MEDUSA
MINOTAUR
MUMMY
VAMPIRE

WEREWOLF
WITCH
WIZARD
WOLF MAN
YETI
ZOMBIE

14

JUST SAYIN'

Give these monsters something to say or think. Then find the hidden STETHOSCOPE, YO-YO, MUG, BANANA, BOOMERANG, CRESCENT MOON, CHILI PEPPER, SPOON, BOOT, and ARTIST'S BRUSH.

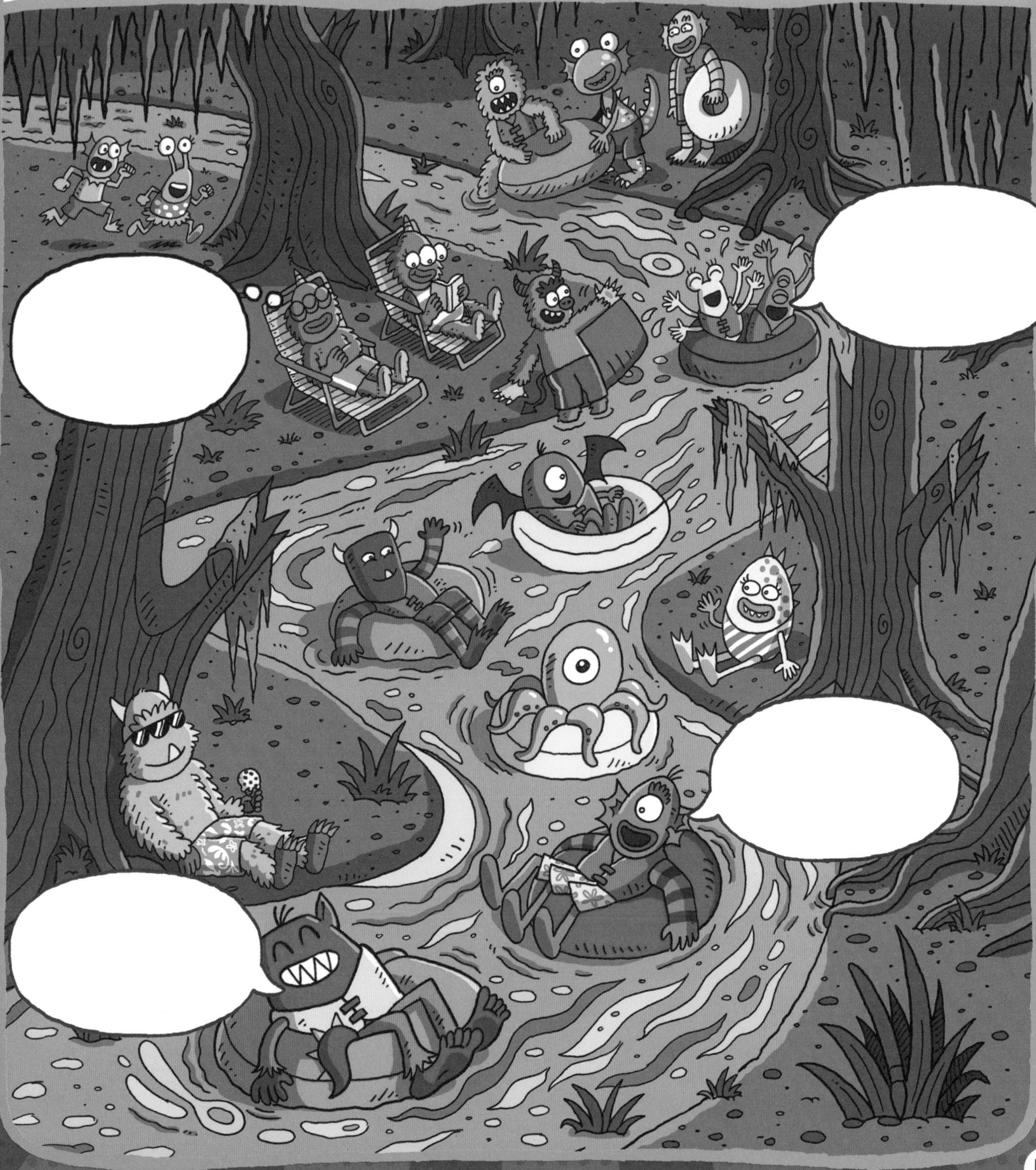

DRAW A MONSTER

Follow the steps to draw a monster.

What did the critics say of Frankenstein's piece of art?

"What a monsterpiece!"

COMIC CREATOR

Create your own monster comic in the blank panels below. What adventures will your monsters have?

DON'T FORGET to sign your comics when you're done!

THE COMIC PAGES

The speech balloons are missing in these cartoons. Can you figure out which sticker belongs with which cartoon?

1

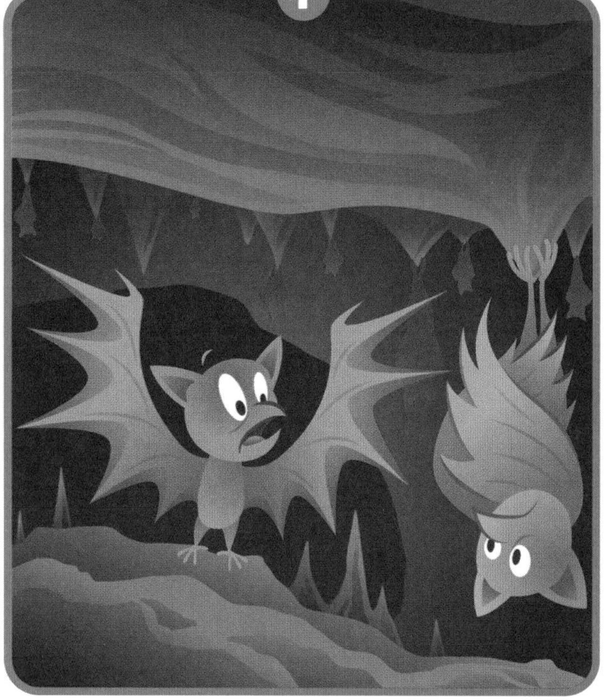

2

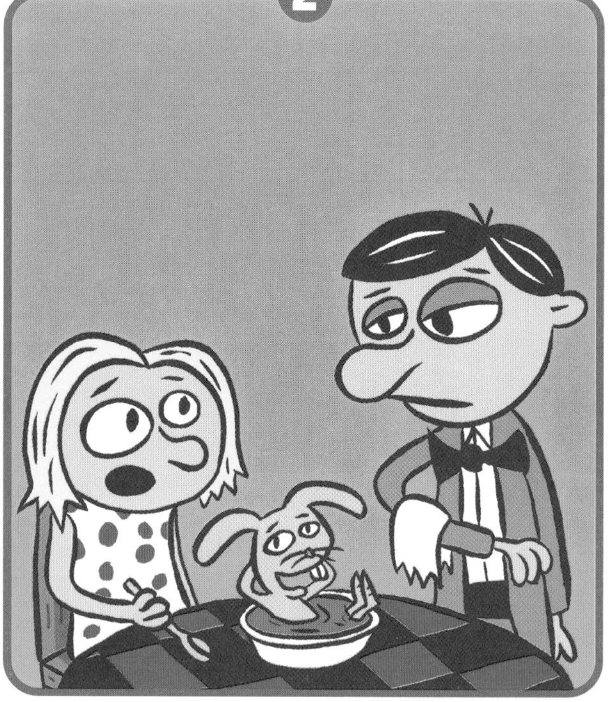

5

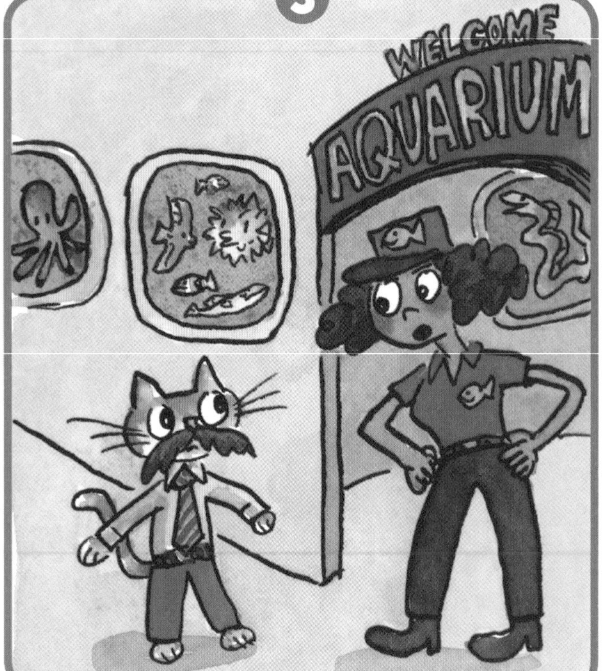
WELCOME
AQUARIUM

6

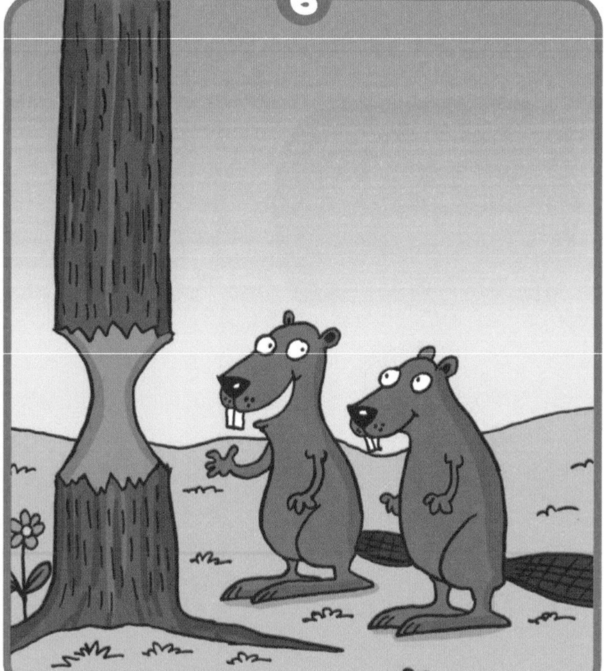

3

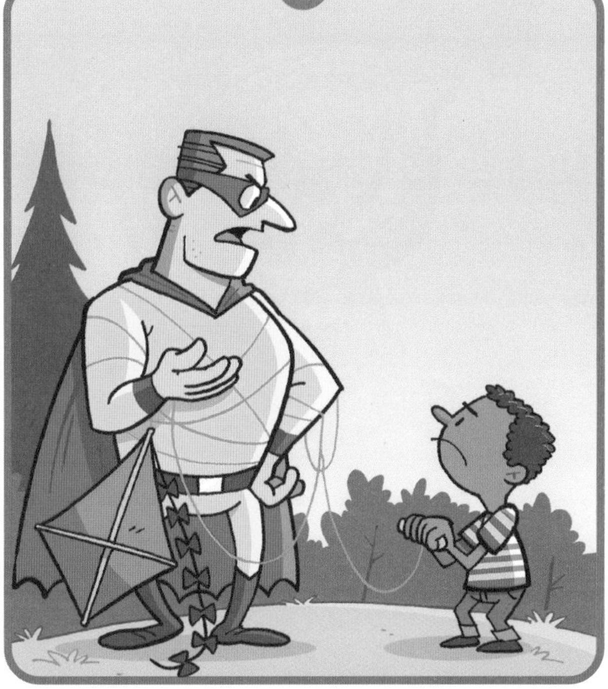

4

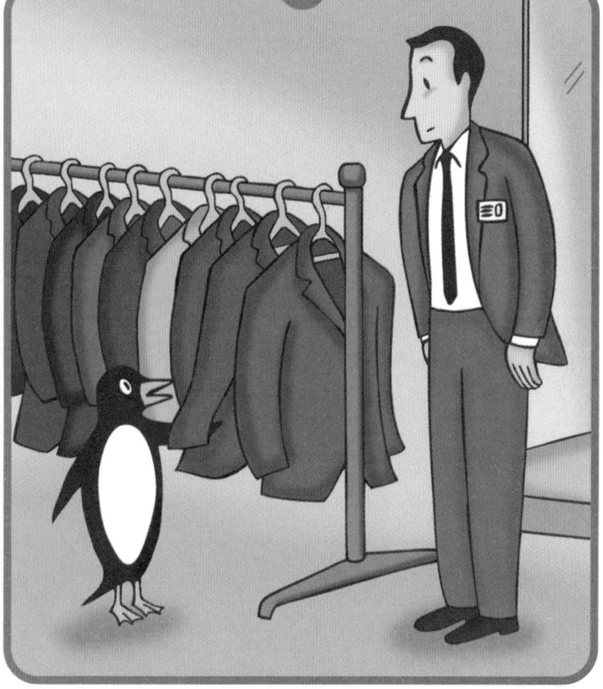

7

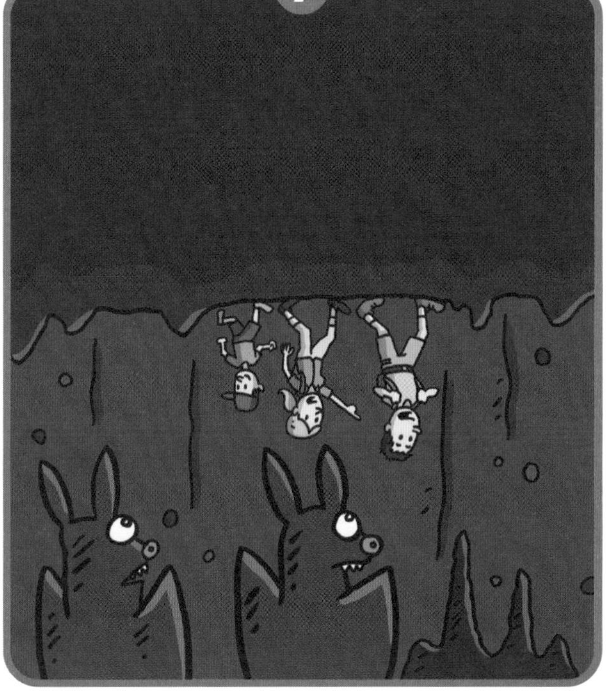

8

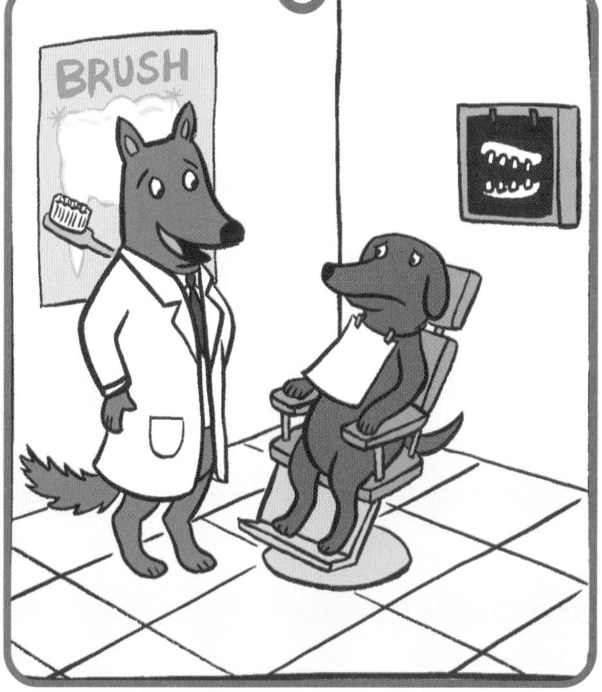
BRUSH

Finish the Comic
Freddy's Superpower

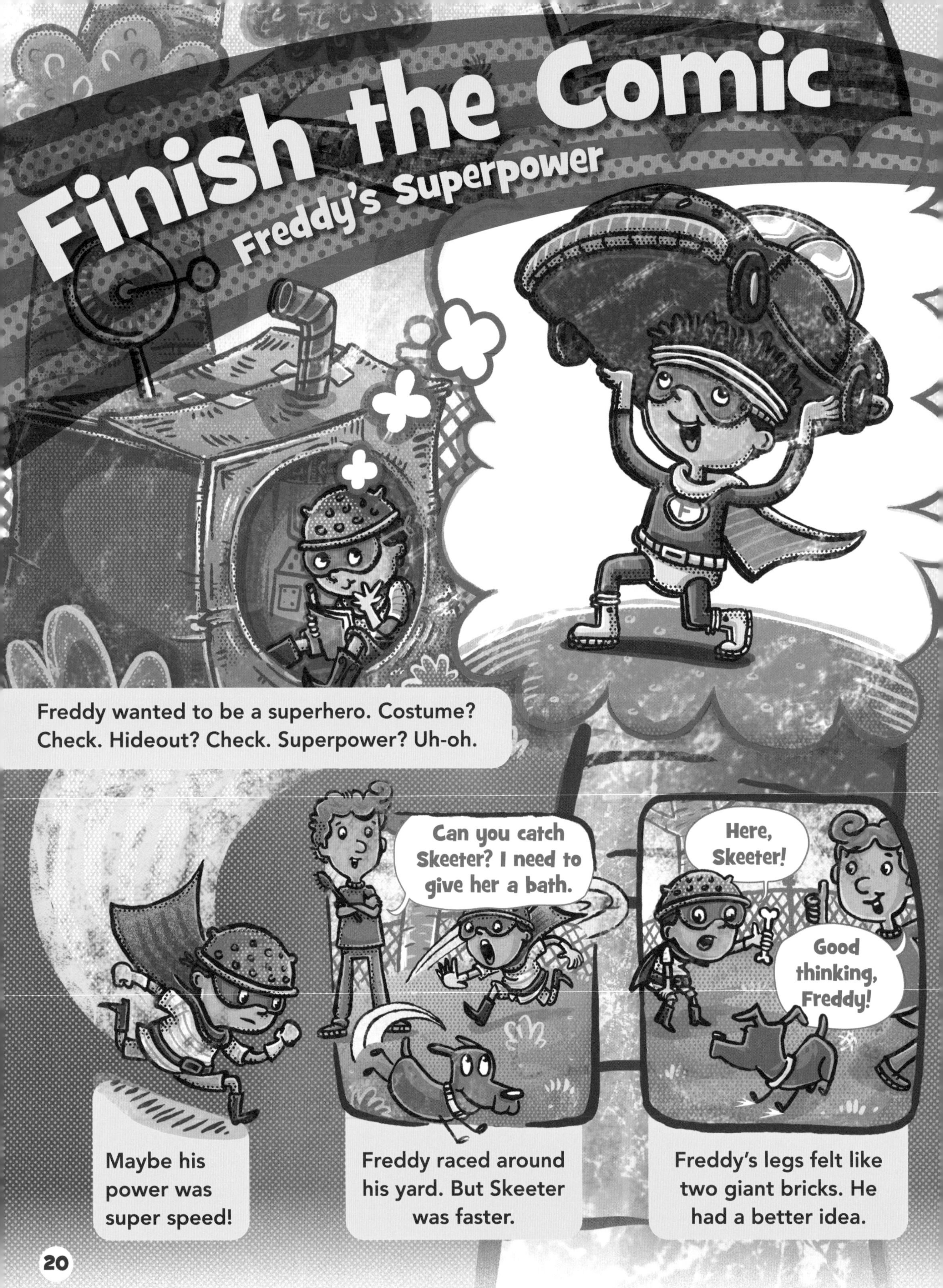
Freddy wanted to be a superhero. Costume? Check. Hideout? Check. Superpower? Uh-oh.
Maybe his power was super speed!
Can you catch Skeeter? I need to give her a bath.
Freddy raced around his yard. But Skeeter was faster.
Here, Skeeter!
Good thinking, Freddy!
Freddy's legs felt like two giant bricks. He had a better idea.

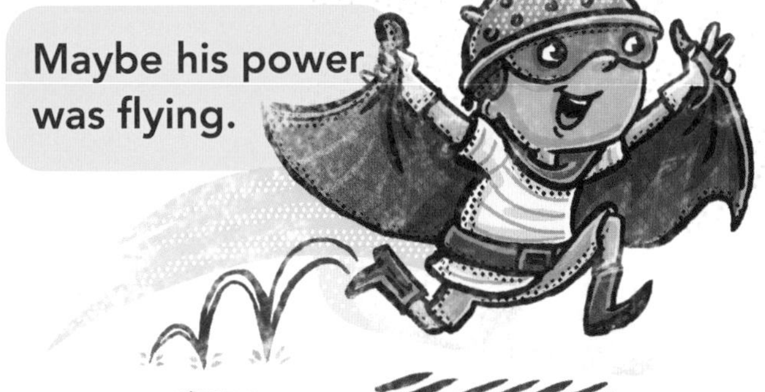
Maybe his power was flying.

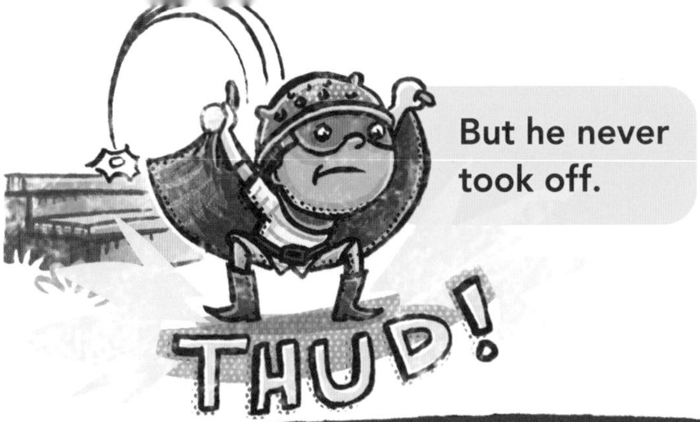
But he never took off.
THUD!

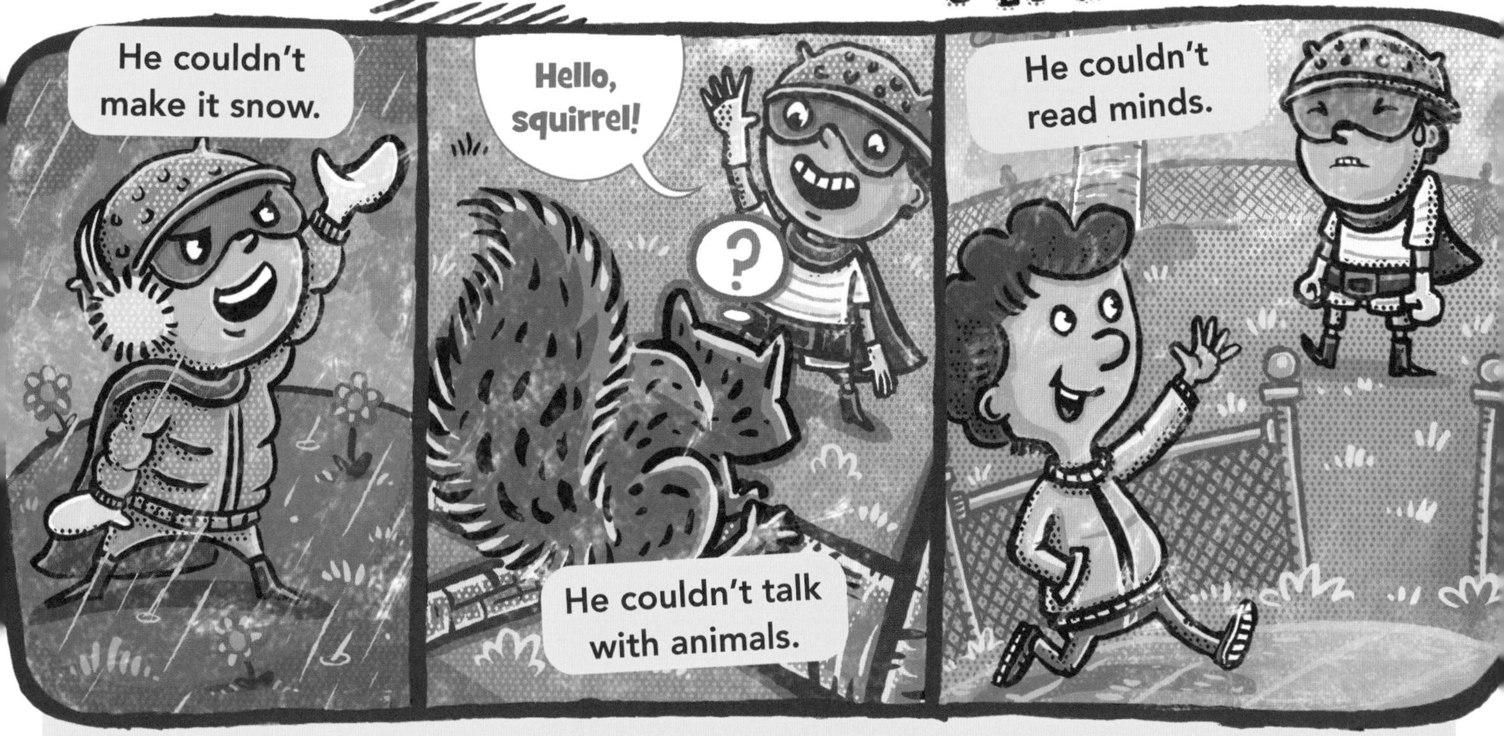
He couldn't make it snow.
Hello, squirrel!
?
He couldn't talk with animals.
He couldn't read minds.

All afternoon, he searched for his superpower.

Then finally he found it.

What could Freddy's superpower be? Draw what you think it is here.

STICKER SOUND EFFECTS

Pow! Wham! Zap! Boom! Bang! Smash! These superheroes have some pretty spectacular powers. Use your stickers to add sound effects to their moves before the dust clears.

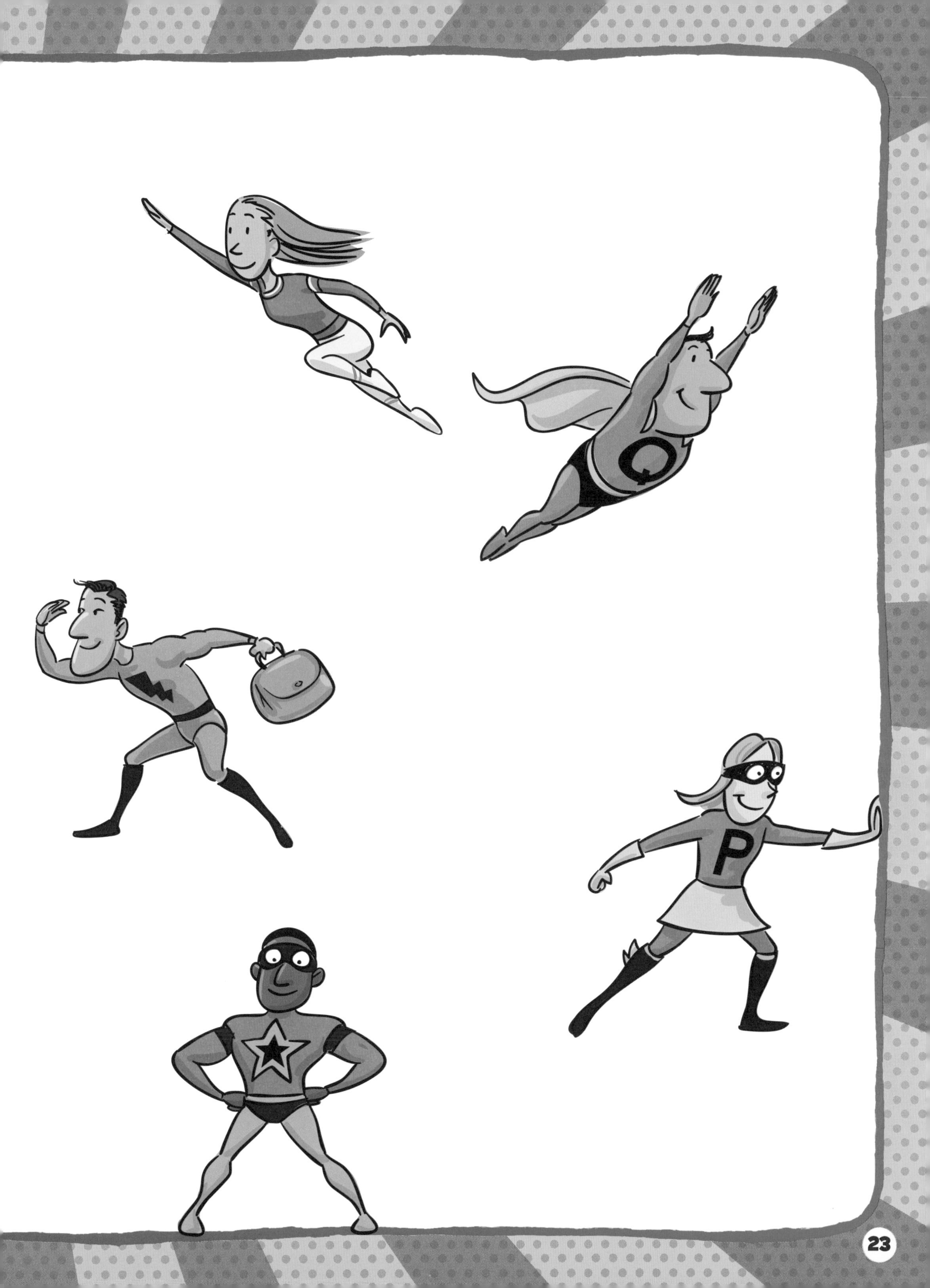

JUST SAYIN'

Give this superhero something to say. Then find the hidden APPLE, DOMINO, DOUGHNUT, FOOTBALL, OPEN BOOK, and RULER.

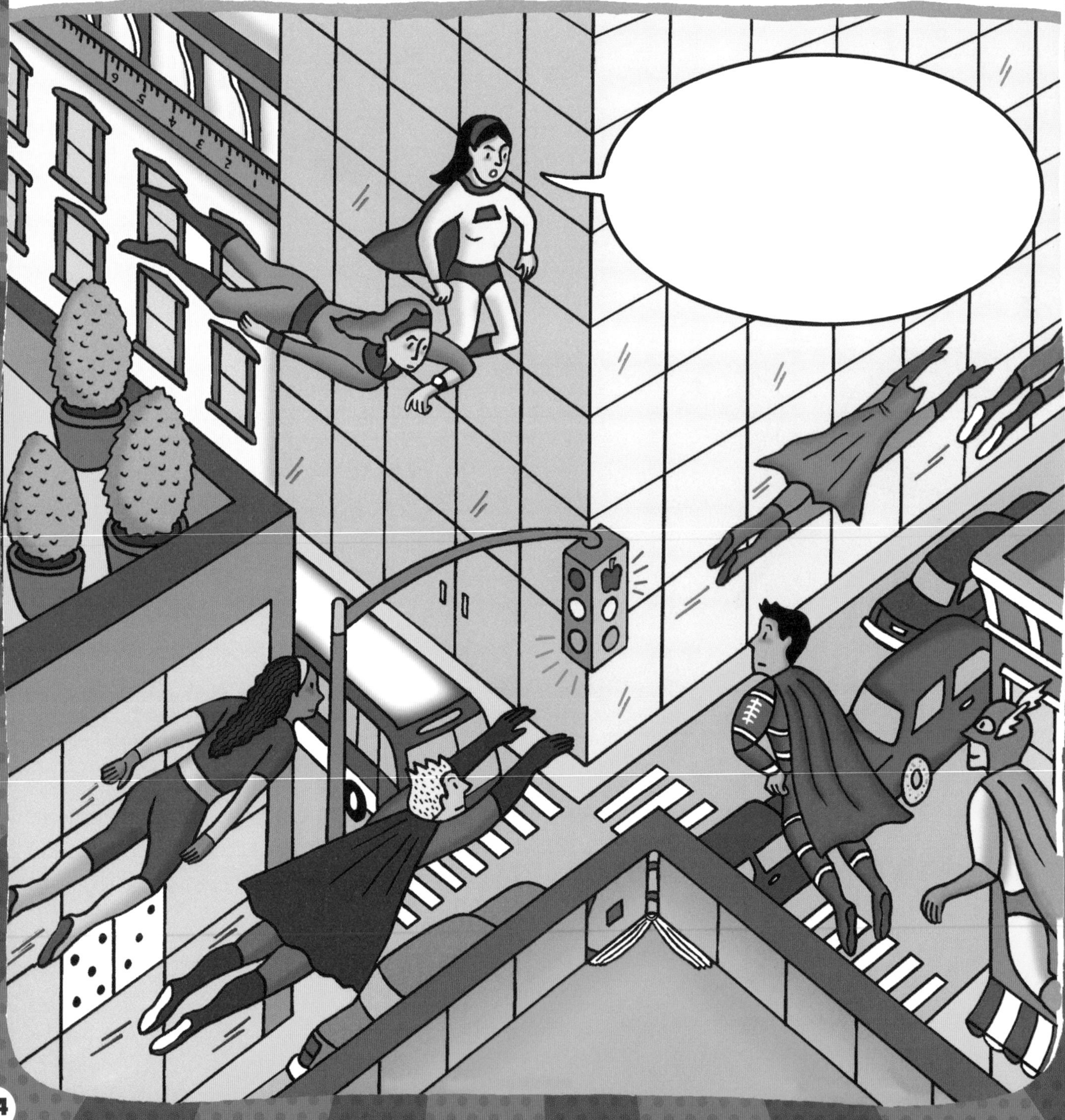

Take this superhero quiz to find out your secret ability.

SUPERPOWER QUIZ

I. **If you had a cape, it would be:**

   a. Red with your emblem on it.
   b. Black.
   c. No capes!

2. **You saved the mayor from your arch nemesis, Dreaded Dynamite. You:**

   a. Stay so the press can get a picture of you.
   b. Slip off into the shadows.
   c. Tell the mayor about your plans for a new indestructible form of transportation.

3. **You are at the Superhero Animal Shelter picking out your new pet sidekick. You choose:**

   a. A hawk; her keen eyesight will come in handy when searching for danger.
   b. A chameleon; he can sneak past your enemies and steal back your plans for the anti-gravity ray.
   c. A lynx; her swift climbing abilities and sharp senses are the perfect protection tools.

4. **The Spark asks you to help her stop Mega Wave. You:**

   a. Don't help because you have too many of your own battles.
   b. Help out! The city is a safer place when people work together.
   c. Help out, but in return, she has to help you stop Dr. Ooze.

5. **Uh-oh! Your arch nemesis's minions have ransacked your hideout. You:**

   a. Barricade your hideout and lie in wait for them to return.
   b. Move to your backup hideout location that is more secure.
   c. Figure out what was taken and infiltrate your arch nemesis's hideout.

If you answered mostly A's, you have the ability to fly! The sky is the limit on your abilities. You love to zoom into the thick of it and show your power to scare away any enemies trying to sneak into your city's shadows.

If you answered mostly B's, you have the ability to be invisible! You love to help people, which is good because no one will see you coming when you take on any nefarious characters. And don't worry, just because you're invisible doesn't mean your impact goes unnoticed.

If you answered mostly C's, you have the ability of mind control! You're the brains behind so many flawless operations. You see beyond the immediate need and do what's best for everyone.

SUPERHERO DOODLES

The sky's the limit when it comes to creating a superhero. Finish drawing these superheroes, then draw some of your own. Don't forget to use your stickers!

SUPER WORD SEARCH

Use your word-searching superpowers to find this superhero's abilities. Only the words in CAPITAL LETTERS are hidden. Then write the leftover letters in order from left to right and top to bottom in the spaces below to find out our superhero's name.

Word List

amazing ~~BRAINPOWER~~
color **CHAMELEON**
mind **CONTROL**
puzzle **DECODER**
ELASTIC body
able to **FLY**
full **FORCE FIELD**
predicts the **FUTURE**
grows **GIANT**
HEALING powers
super **HEARING**
turns **INVISIBLE**
astounding **JUMPER**
LASER eyes
casts **MAGIC** spells
incredible **MEMORY**
shape **SHIFTER**
SPACE traveler
fantastic **SPEED**
TIME traveler
WATER breather
WIZARD skills
X-RAY vision

W	A	T	E	R	M	C	O	N	T	R	O	L
R	C	H	A	M	E	L	E	O	N	I	R	I
E	H	E	A	R	I	N	G	N	B	C	M	R
T	E	D	L	E	I	F	E	C	R	O	F	E
F	F	U	T	U	R	E	D	T	A	I	B	L
I	E	L	B	I	S	I	V	N	I	M	Y	G
H	L	A	W	E	S	O	M	A	N	A	R	N
S	A	S	P	E	E	D	E	I	P	G	E	I
S	S	Y	R	O	M	E	M	G	O	I	S	L
U	T	P	E	S	P	A	C	E	W	C	A	A
W	I	Z	A	R	D	R	H	E	E	F	L	E
R	C	R	E	P	M	U	J	O	R	G	L	H
D	E	C	O	D	E	R	U	Y	X	R	A	Y

His name is __ __. __ __ __ __ __ __ __ __ __ __ __ __ __ __ __ __

__ __ __ __ __ __ __ __ __ __ __ __ __ __!

28

HIDDEN PICTURES

Find the hidden objects in the comic-book store.

crescent moon

caterpillar

boot

fork

ring

nail

sailboat

sock

bowl

lollipop

closed umbrella

ice-cream bar

ladder

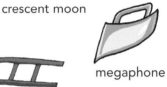
megaphone

golf club

ladle

snake

drinking straw

29

DRAW A SUPERMOBILE

Follow the steps to draw a supermobile.

1 **2** **3**

4 **5**

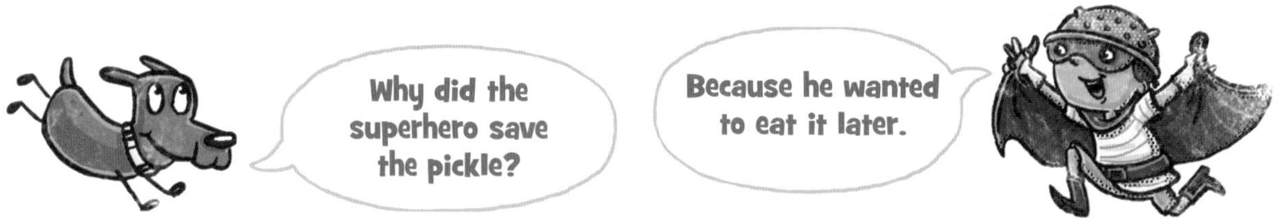

Why did the superhero save the pickle?

Because he wanted to eat it later.

COMIC CREATOR

Create your own superhero comic inside the panels below. What or whom is your superhero going to save?

THE COMIC PAGES

The speech balloons are missing in these cartoons. Can you figure out which sticker belongs with which cartoon?

1

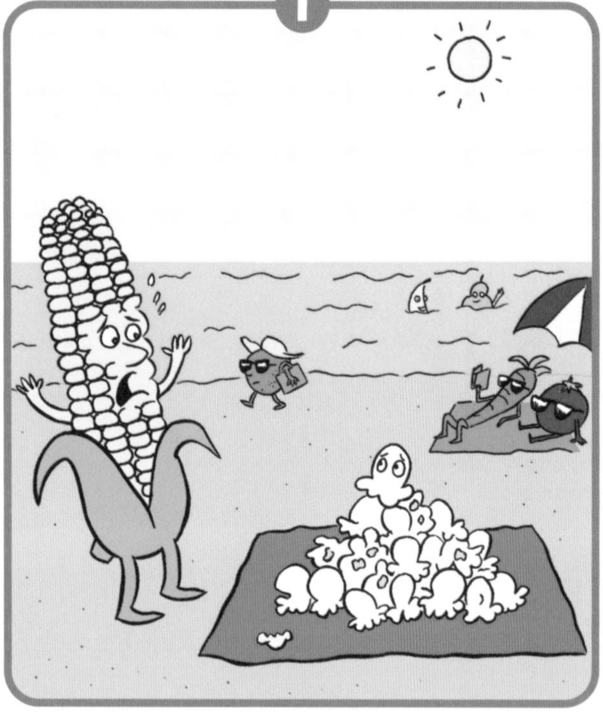

2

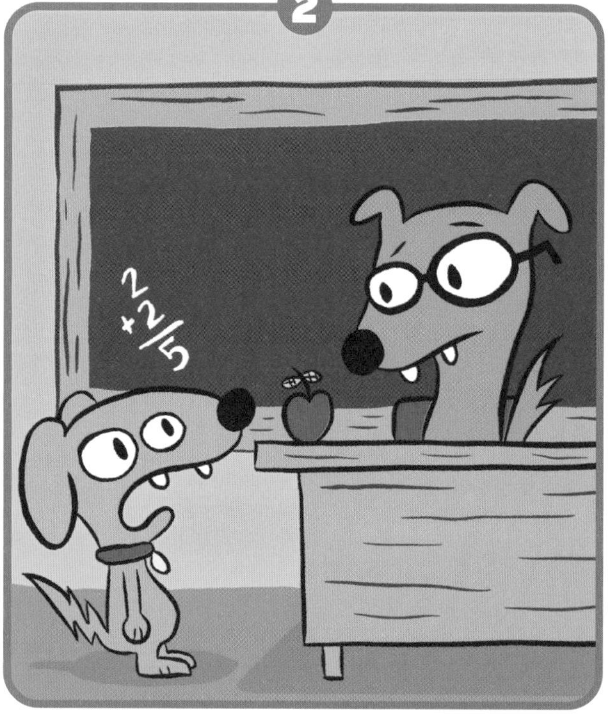
2
+2
5

5

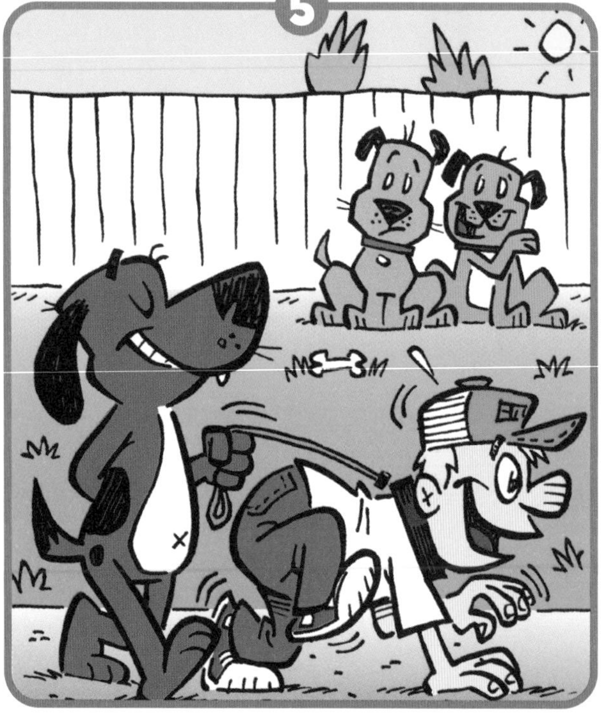

6

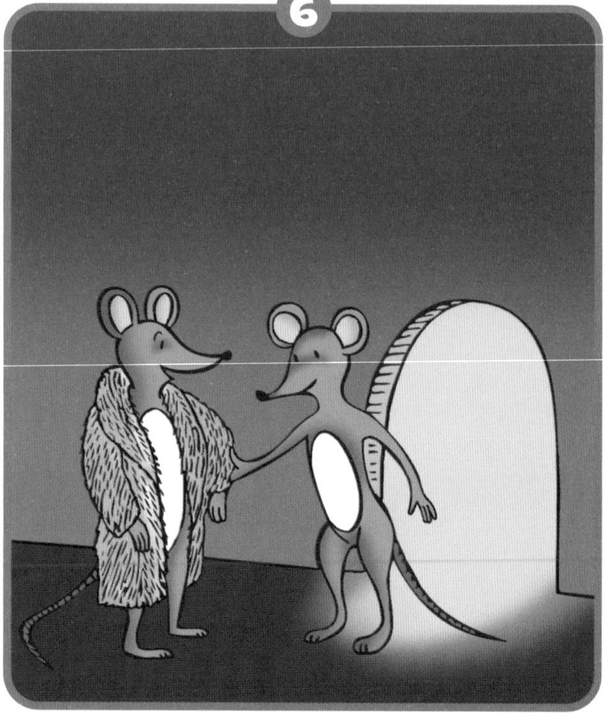

3

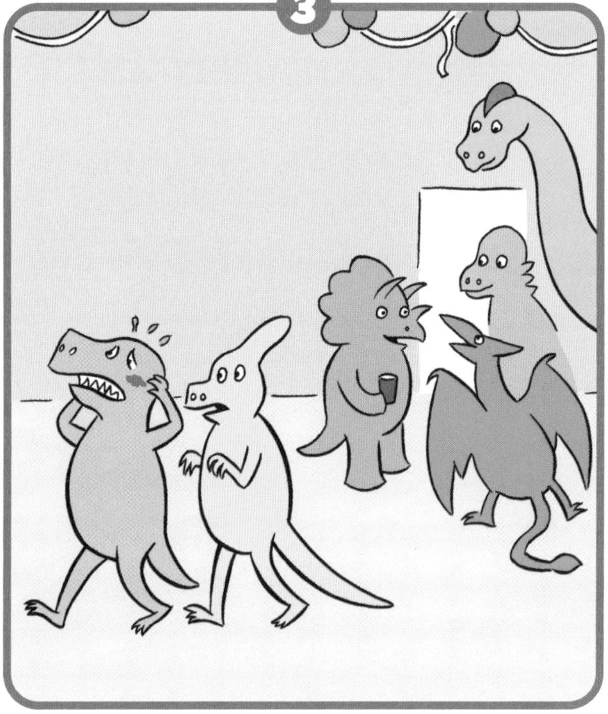

4

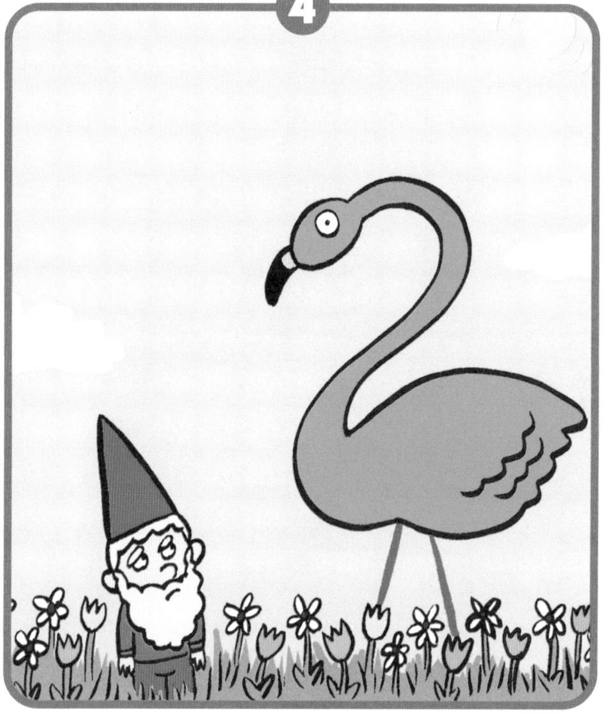

7

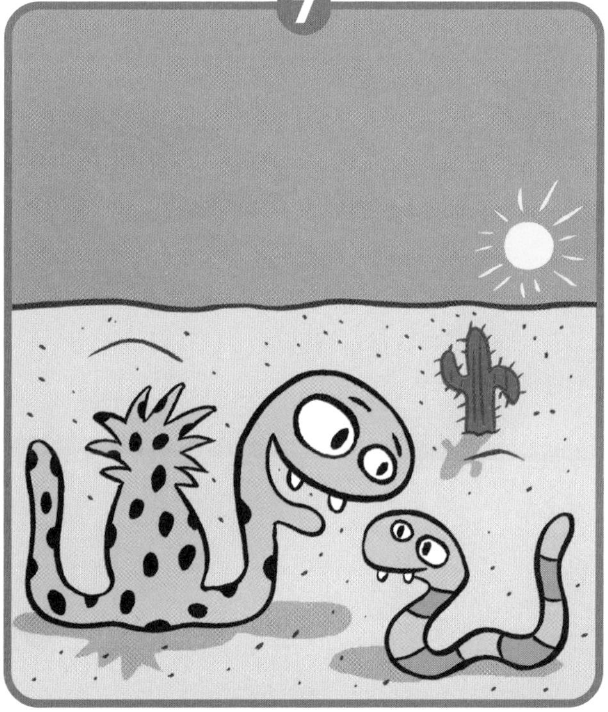

8

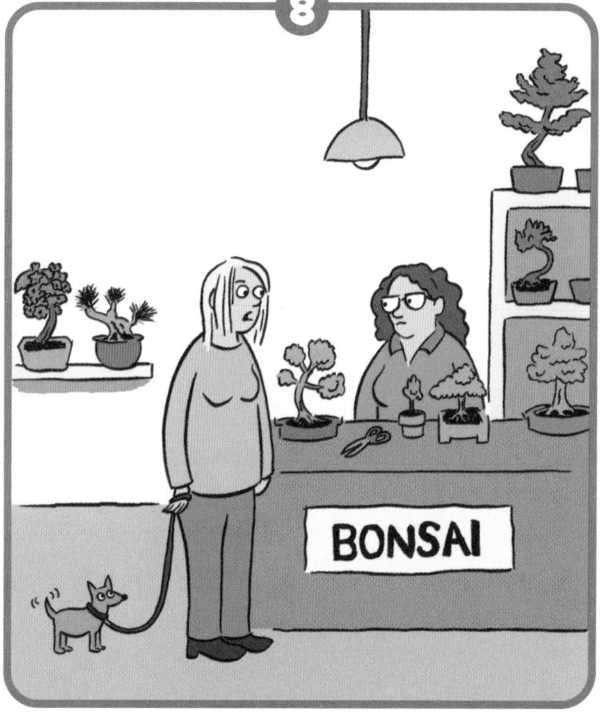
BONSAI

Finish the Comic
The Bug Race

What do you think will happen at the race? Write in the missing pieces in the blank speech bubbles.

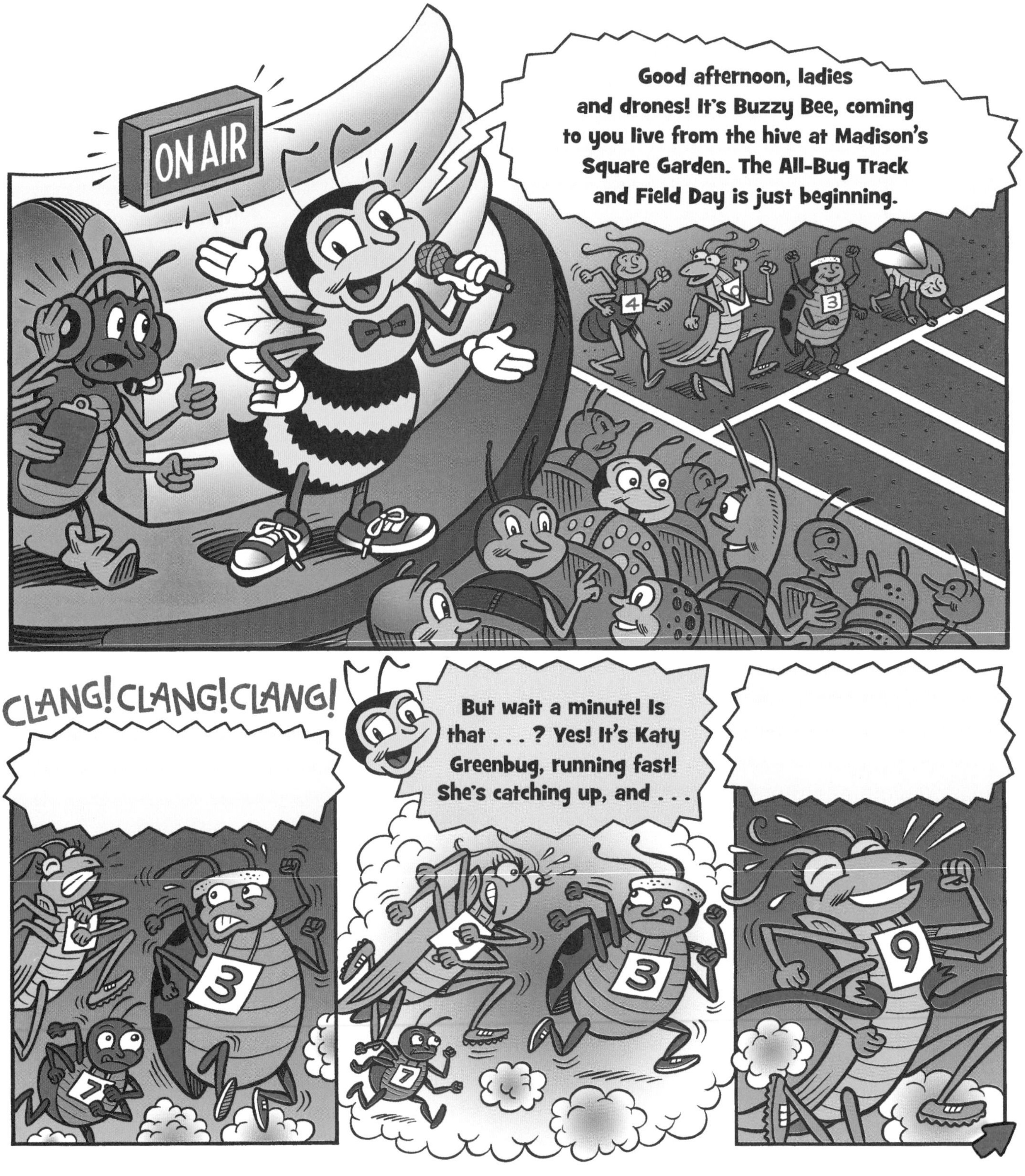

Good afternoon, ladies and drones! It's Buzzy Bee, coming to you live from the hive at Madison's Square Garden. The All-Bug Track and Field Day is just beginning.
ON AIR
CLANG! CLANG! CLANG!
But wait a minute! Is that . . . ? Yes! It's Katy Greenbug, running fast! She's catching up, and . . .

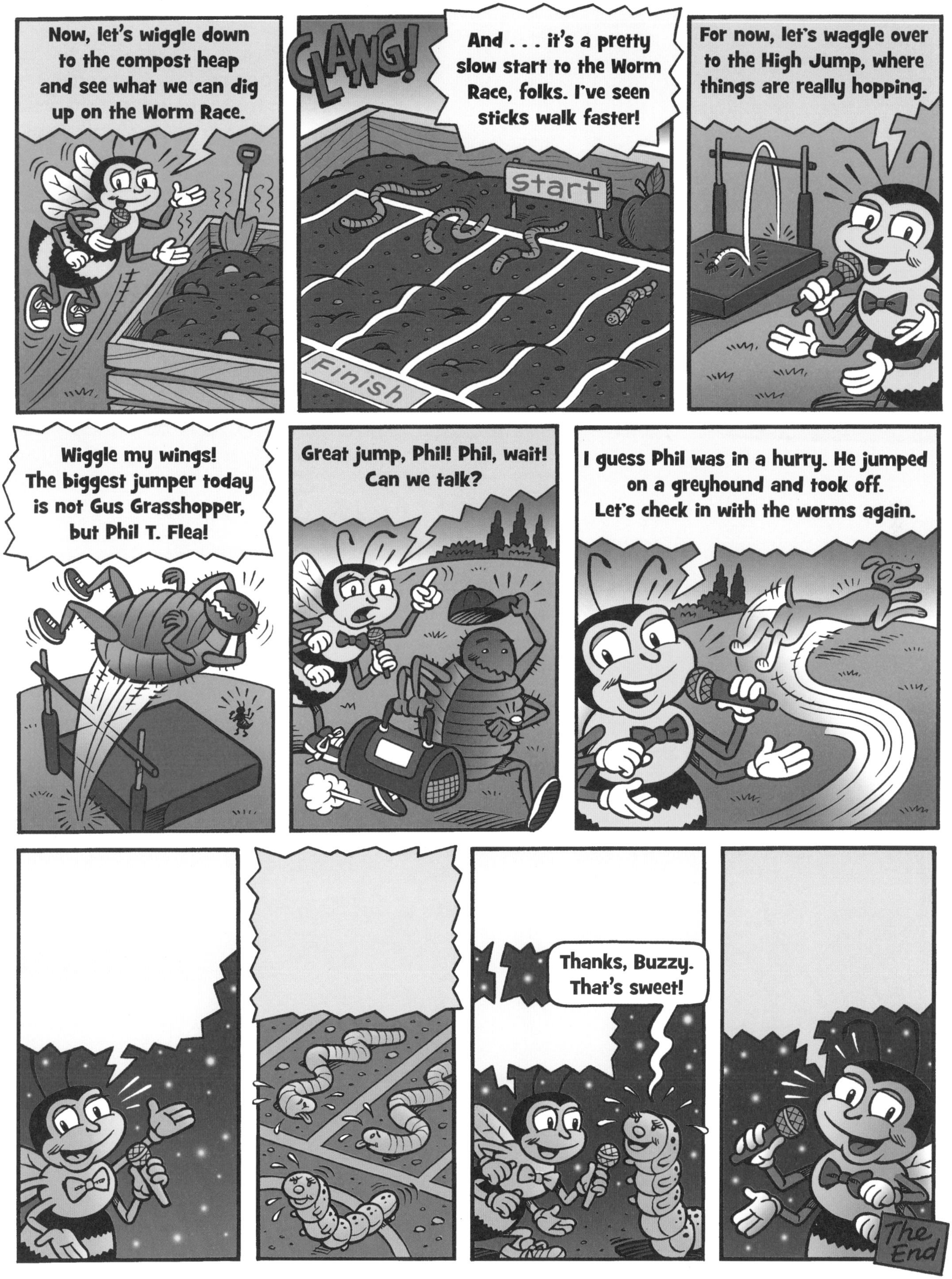
Now, let's wiggle down to the compost heap and see what we can dig up on the Worm Race.
CLANG!
And . . . it's a pretty slow start to the Worm Race, folks. I've seen sticks walk faster!
Start
Finish
For now, let's waggle over to the High Jump, where things are really hopping.
Wiggle my wings! The biggest jumper today is not Gus Grasshopper, but Phil T. Flea!
Great jump, Phil! Phil, wait! Can we talk?
I guess Phil was in a hurry. He jumped on a greyhound and took off. Let's check in with the worms again.
Thanks, Buzzy. That's sweet!
The End

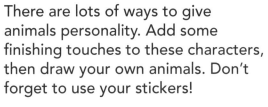

There are lots of ways to give animals personality. Add some finishing touches to these characters, then draw your own animals. Don't forget to use your stickers!

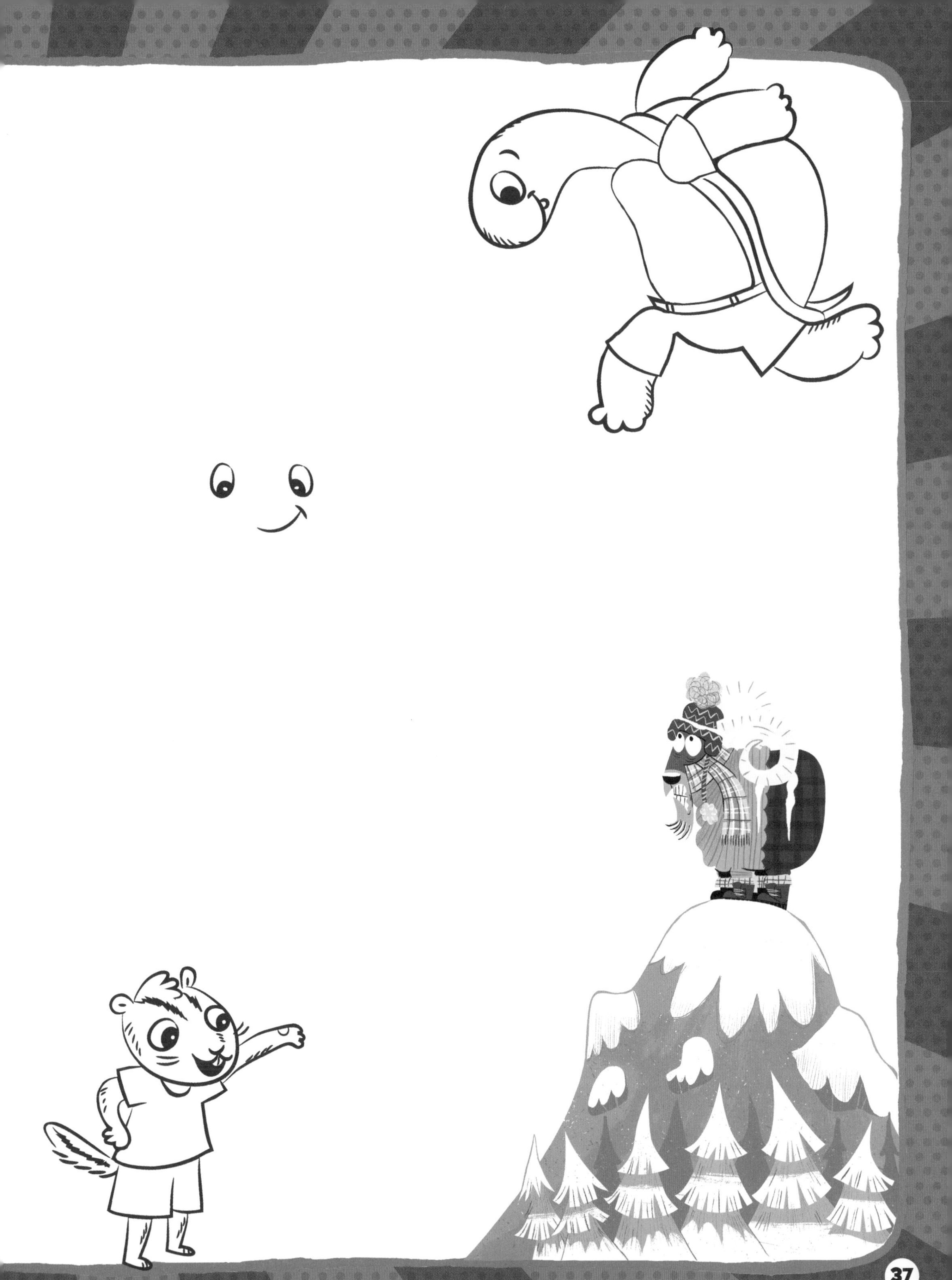

FUNNY FILL-IN

Don't be a chicken; crack up with this comedy coop troop. Come up with your own jokes for these chickens to say.

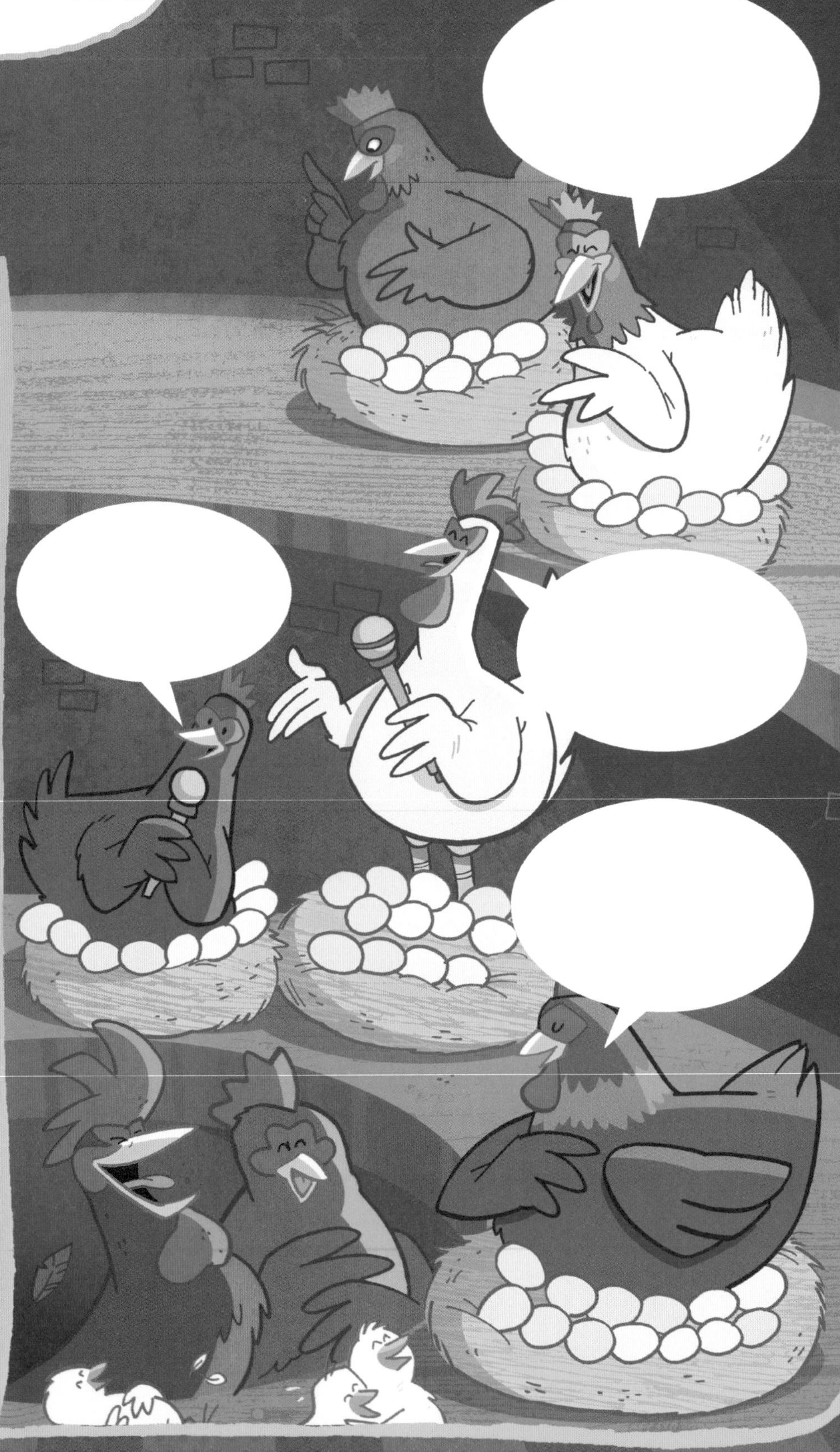

Take time to unscramble these egg-cellent jokes.

Which birds are sad?

EBUL SAJY

What can turkeys use to play an instrument?

DISTUMRCKS

What do you give a sick bird?

TENTMEWET

What are smarter than talking birds?

SINGLEPL SEBE

What do you get when you cross centipedes with parrots?

KEAWLI-KEATLIS

ANIMAL MIX-UP

Mix and match these animal characteristics to create your own animal hybrids. What would your animal hybrids be called? Draw them below.

This animal **flies**, . . .	has **three horns**, . . .	and lives in a **cave**.
This animal **swims**, . . .	has **long, floppy ears**, . . .	and lives in the **jungle**.
This animal is **giant**, . . .	is **rainbow-colored**, . . .	and lives **underground**.
This animal is **tiny**, . . .	has **eight legs**, . . .	and lives in the **artic**.
This animal is **shy**, . . .	is covered in **spots**, . . .	and lives in the **library**.

CREATURE CODE

Do you know what these baby animals are called? Use the code to find out.

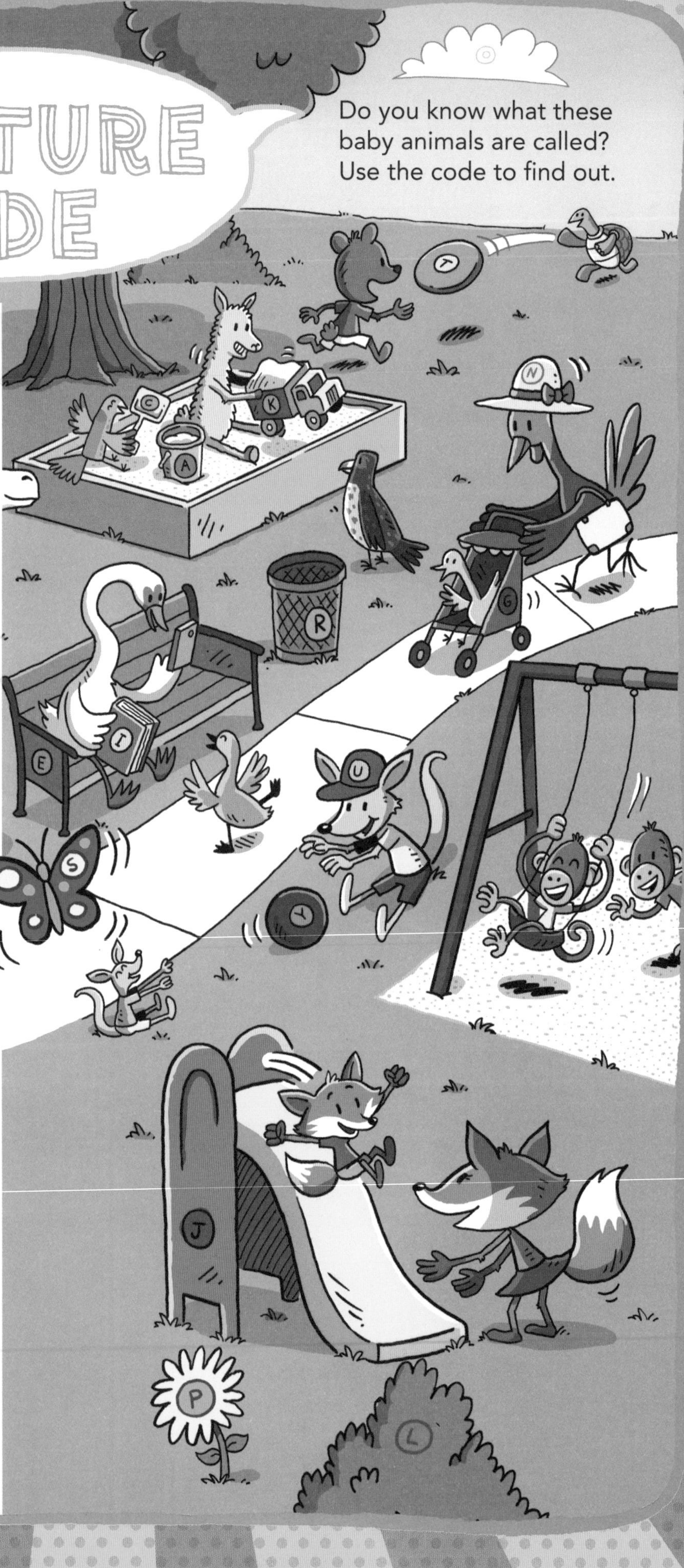

T
N
C
K
A
R
G
I
E
U
S
Y
J
P
L

1 BABY KANGAROO

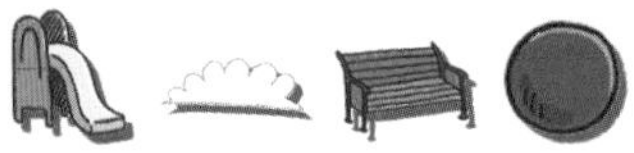

2 BABY TURKEY

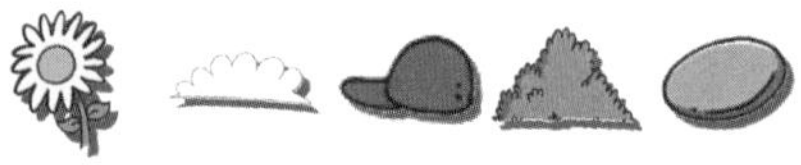

3 BABY FOX

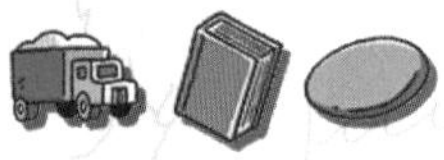

4 BABY HAWK

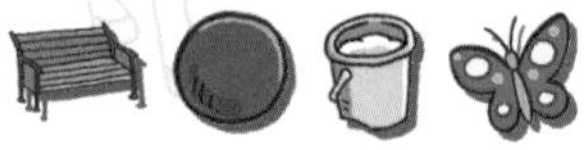

5 BABY SWAN

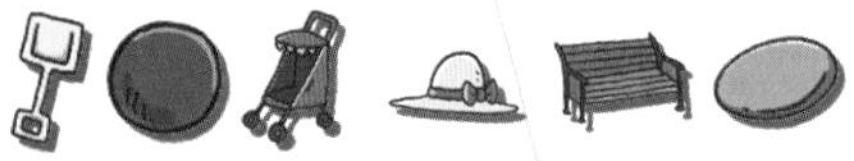

6 BABY LLAMA

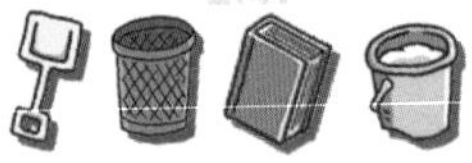

Bonus!

What did the cat say after telling a joke?

"I'm just

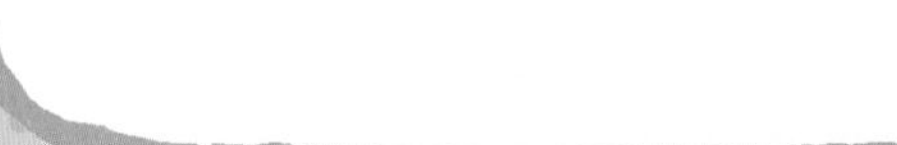 !"

JUST SAYIN'

Give the dentist something to say. Give the shark something to think. Then find the hidden BANANA, BASEBALL CAP, BOOK, MAGNIFYING GLASS, and SOCK.

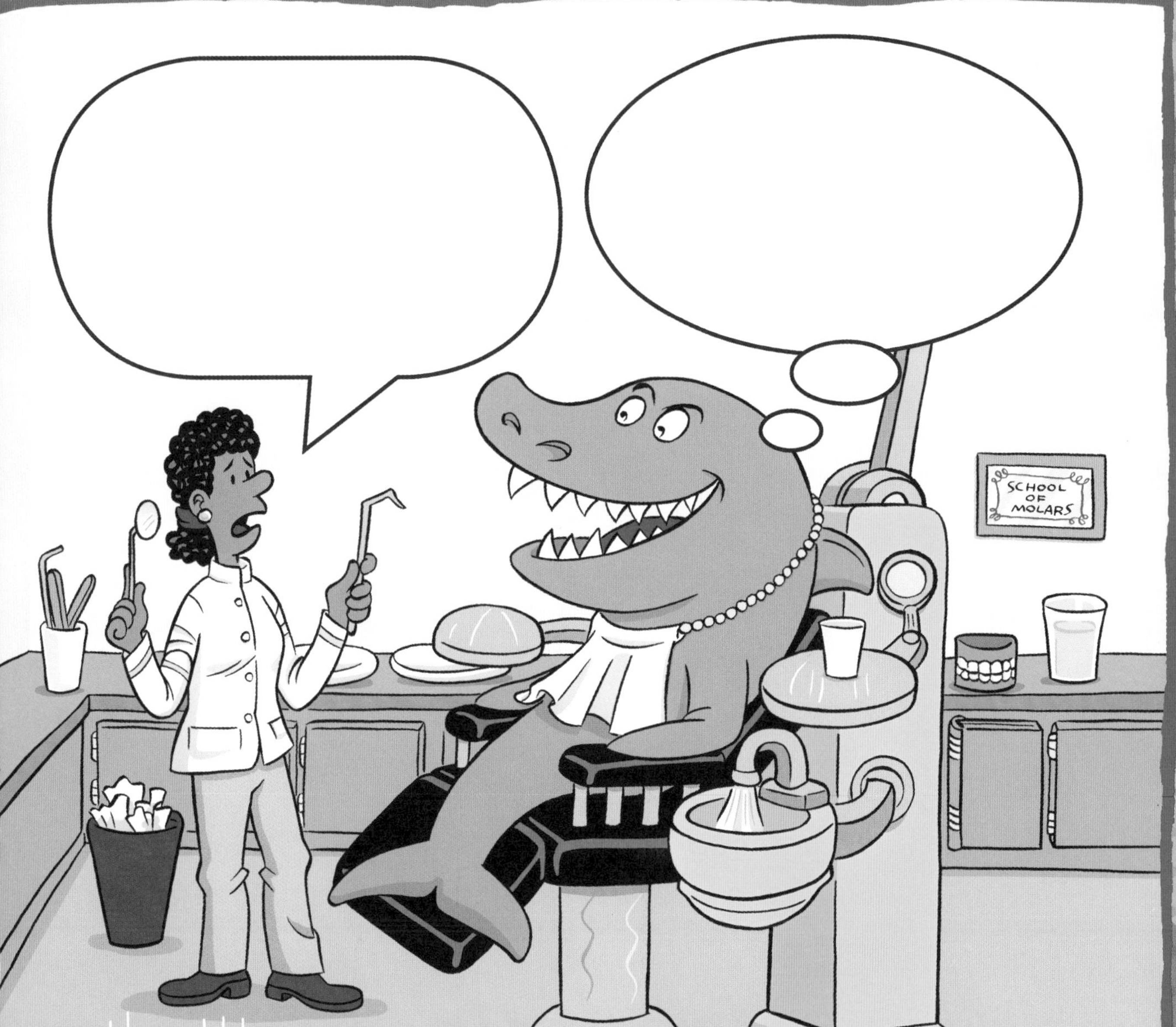
SCHOOL OF MOLARS

DRAW A GRUMPY BEAR

Follow these steps to draw a bear.

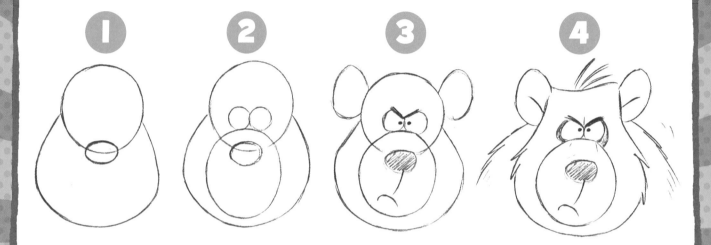

What do you call a bear with no socks?

Bearfoot

COMIC CREATOR

Create your own animal comic. Will your animals live in the wild or act like humans?

THE COMIC PAGES

The speech balloons are missing in these cartoons. Can you figure out which sticker belongs with which cartoon?

1

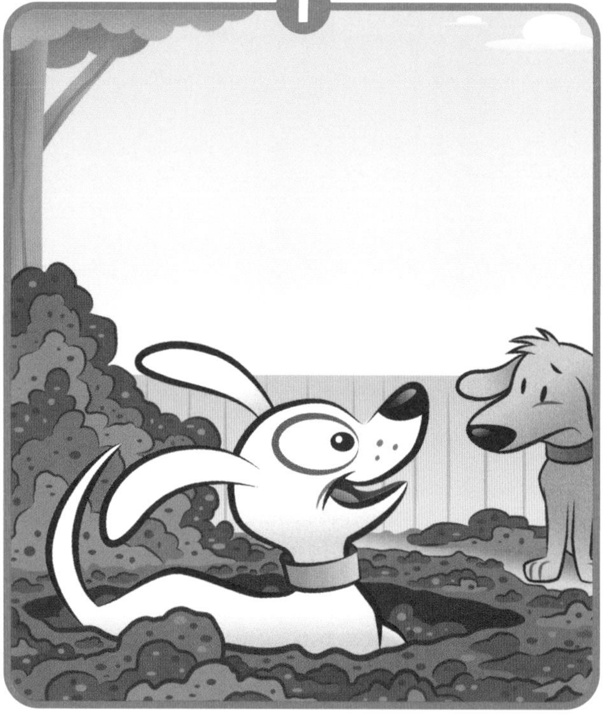

2

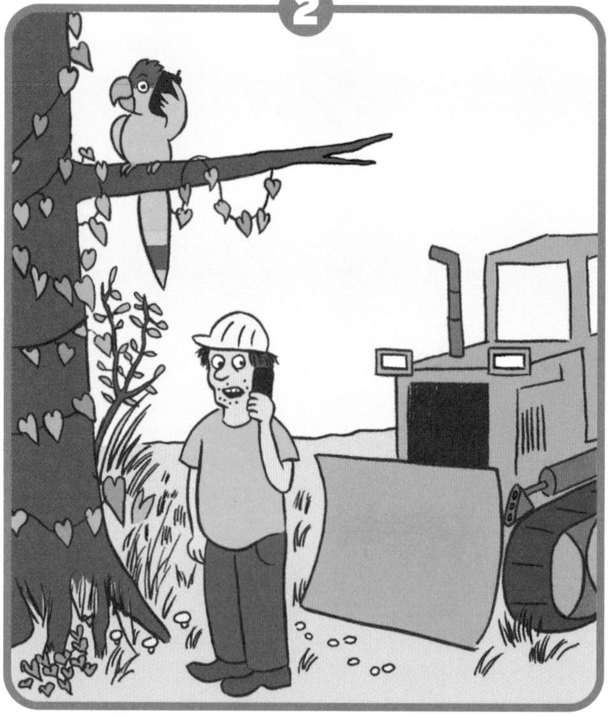

5

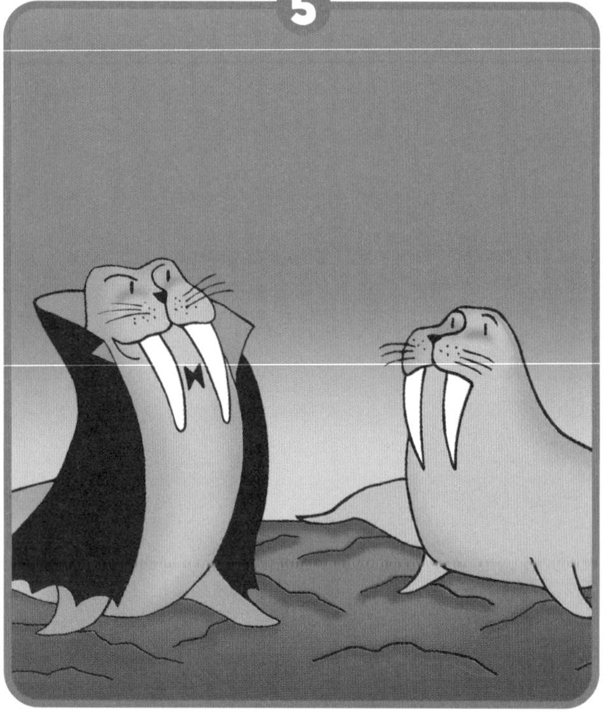

6

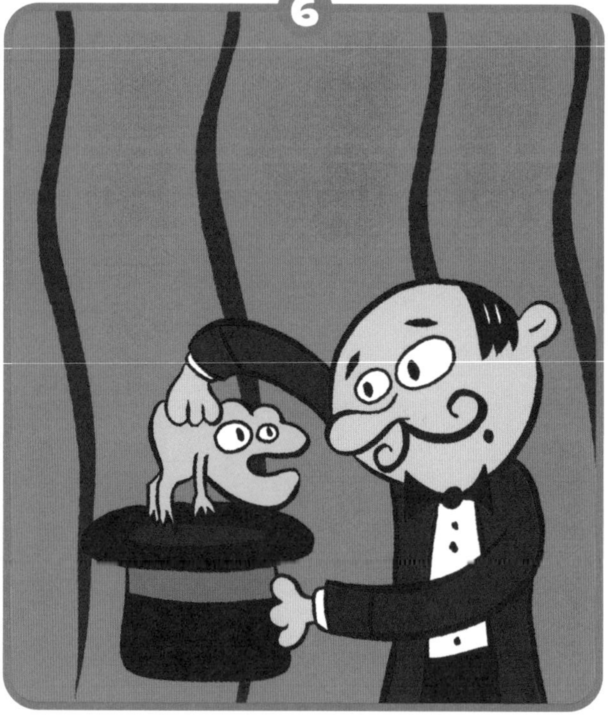

Finish the Comic
The Lonely Dragon

One day, Frances the dragon went into town to see if he could find a friend.

What do you think will happen next?
Write the missing pieces in the blank speech bubbles.

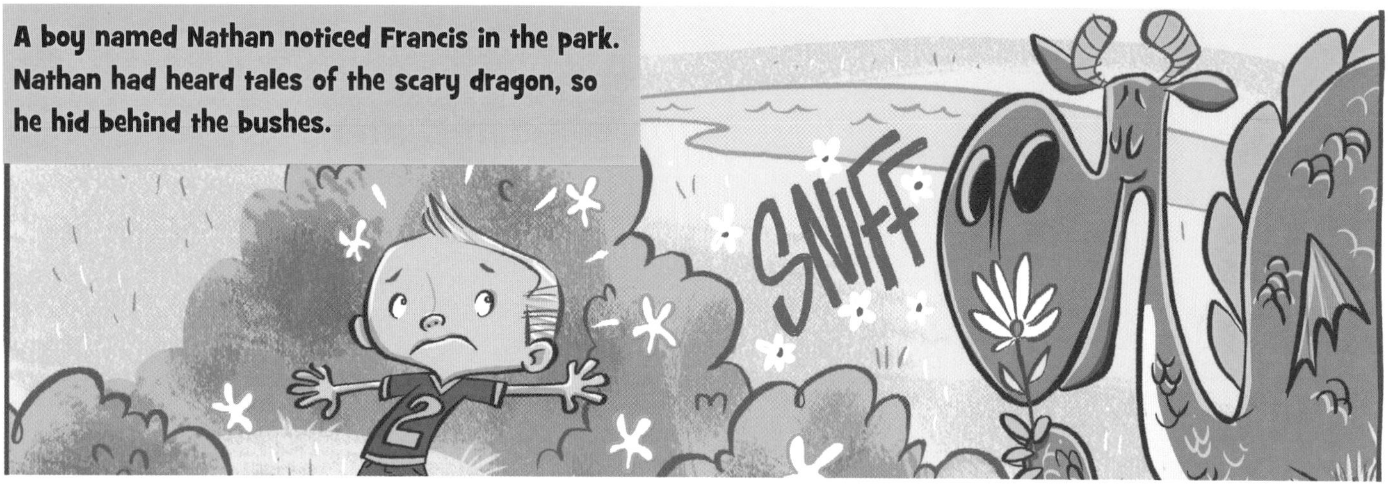
A boy named Nathan noticed Francis in the park. Nathan had heard tales of the scary dragon, so he hid behind the bushes.
SNIFF

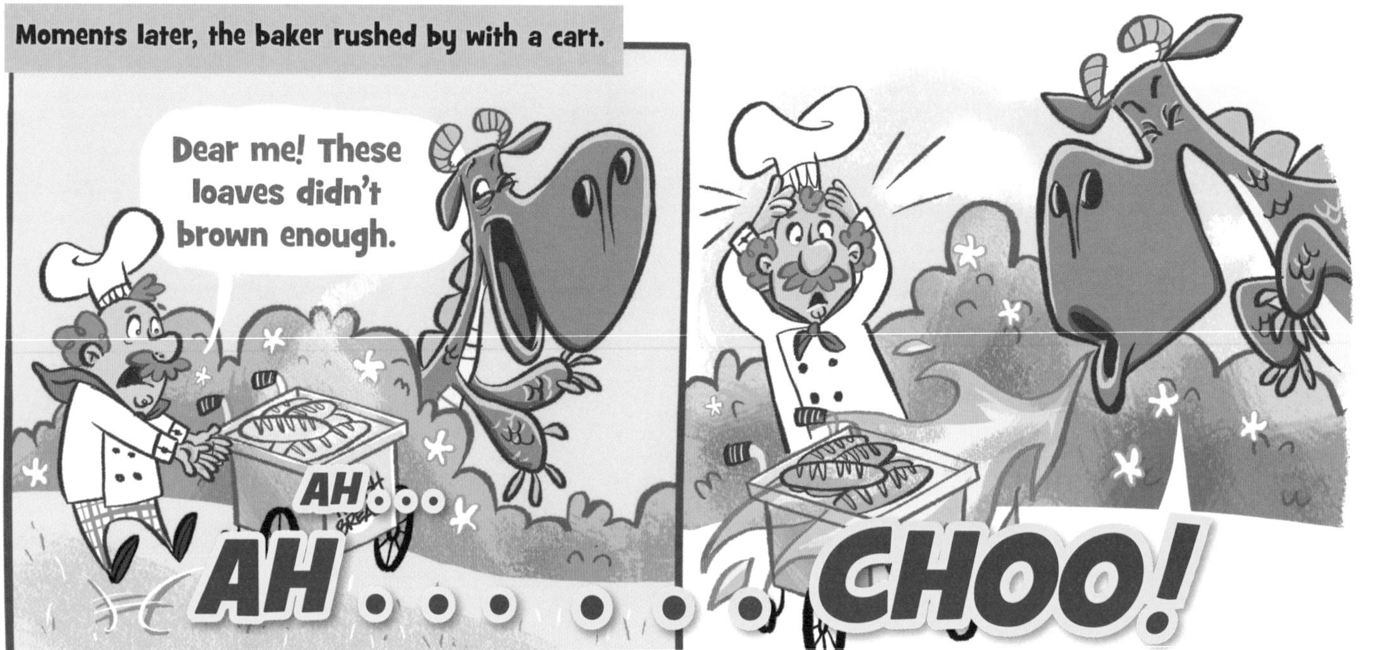
Moments later, the baker rushed by with a cart.
Dear me! These loaves didn't brown enough.
AH...
AH . . . . . . CHOO!

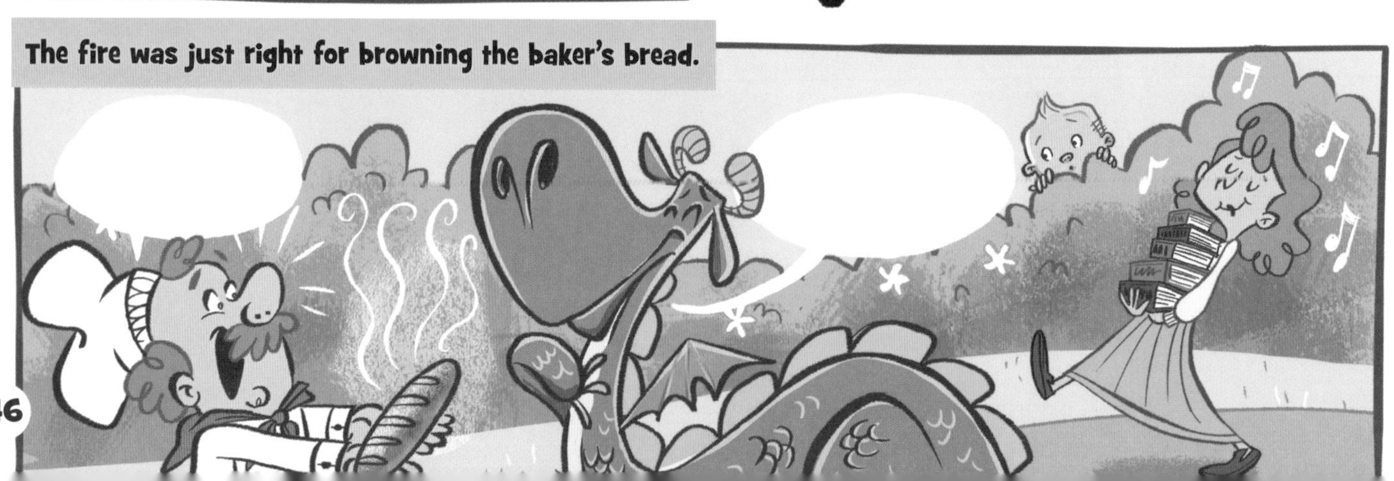
The fire was just right for browning the baker's bread.

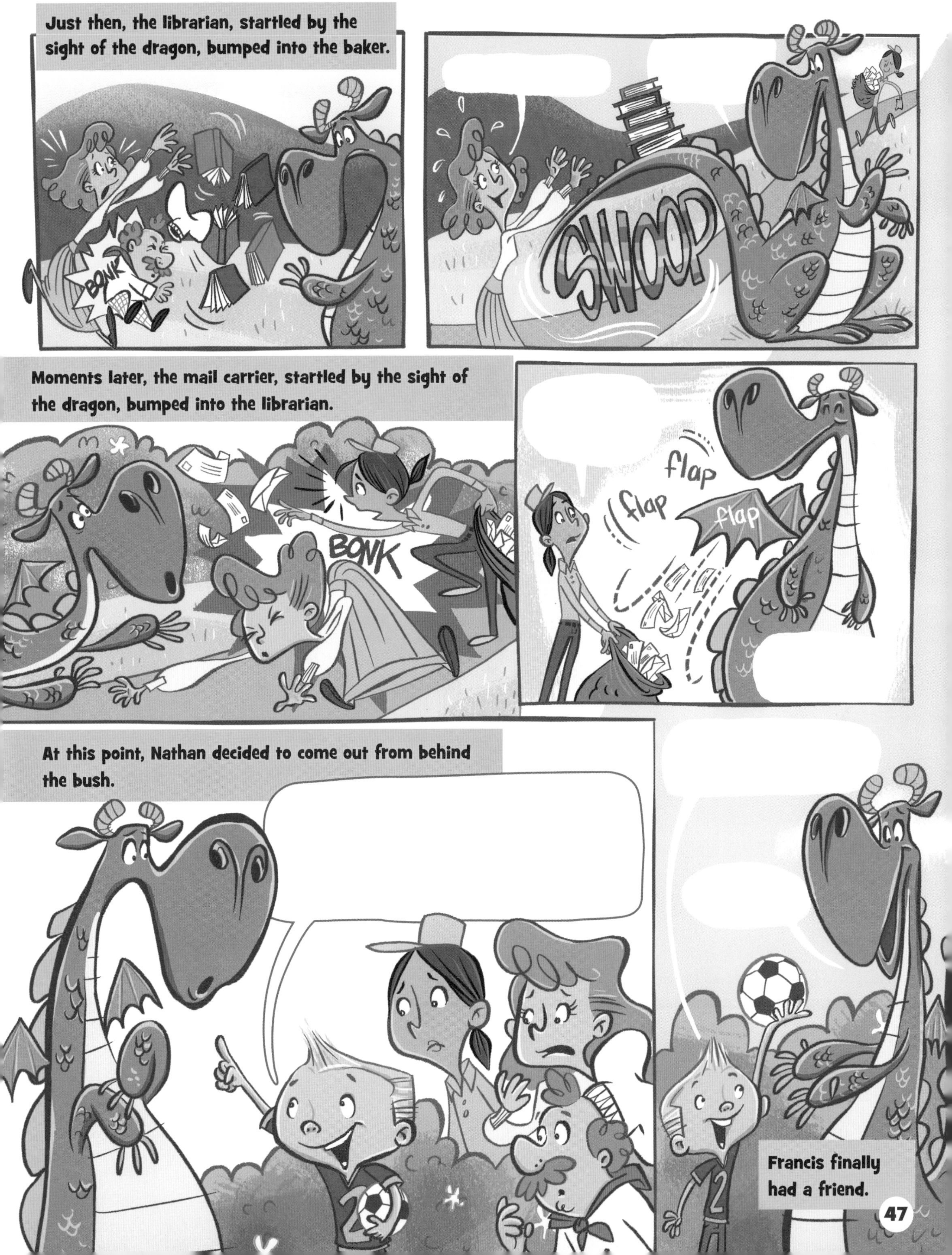
Just then, the librarian, startled by the sight of the dragon, bumped into the baker.
BONK
SWOOP
Moments later, the mail carrier, startled by the sight of the dragon, bumped into the librarian.
BONK
flap
flap
flap
At this point, Nathan decided to come out from behind the bush.
Francis finally had a friend.

MYTHICAL DOODLES

Motion lines give the impression that a character or object is moving. And writing the sound of the movement—or onomatopoeia—with the motion lines creates an even bigger impact!

flap
flap
flap

Practice these techniques below, then draw some of your own characters. Don't forget to use your stickers!

JUST SAYIN'

Give these creatures something to say. Then help each of them get home from the Mythical Creatures Convention.

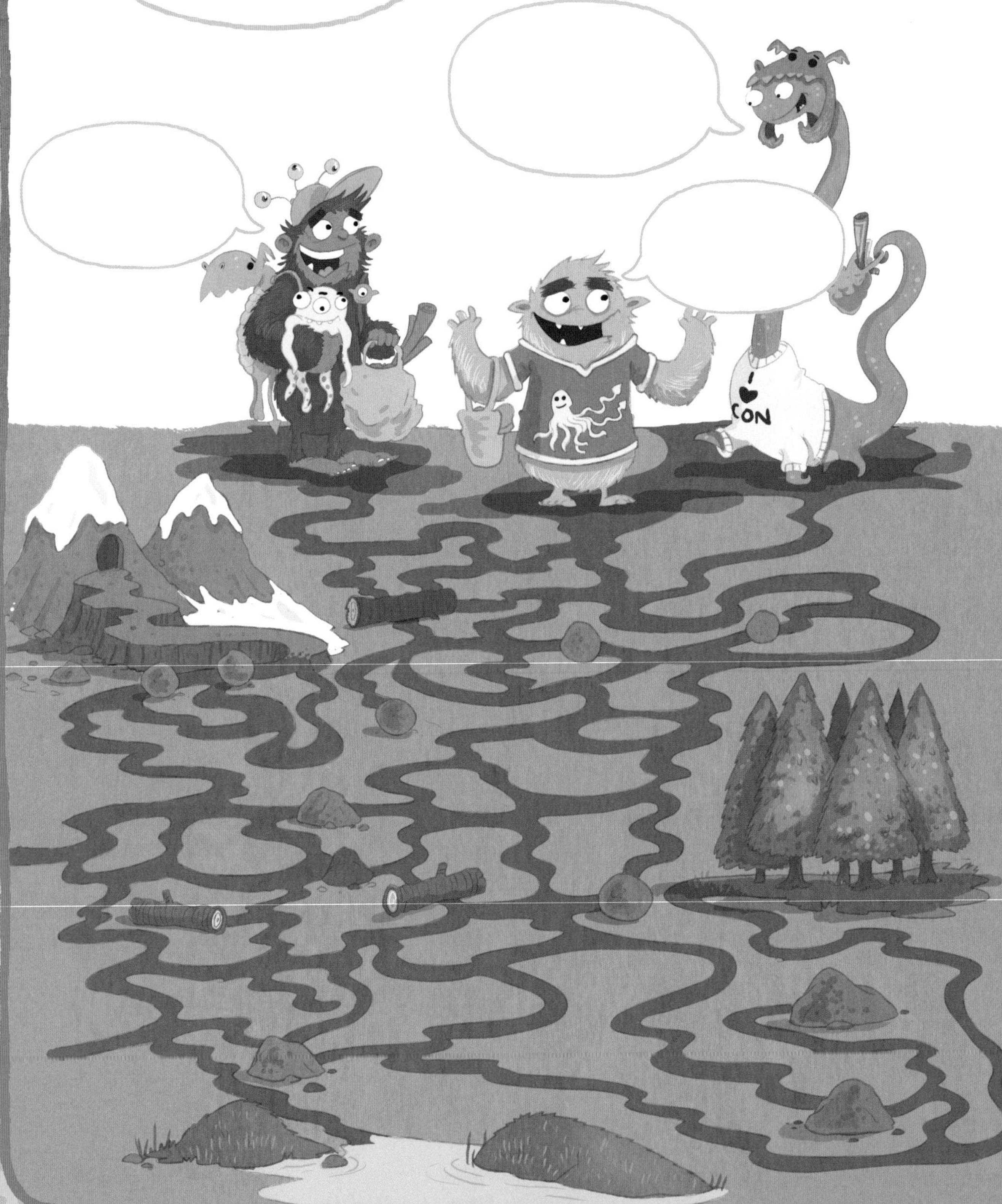
I ♥ CON

CREATURE CREATION

Create your own mythical creature by answering these questions. Then draw your creature and give it a silly caption.

What is your creature's name? _____

How many exist? _____

Can it fly? Breathe fire? Become invisible? _____

Where does your creature live? _____

How many people have seen your creature? _____

Does it have feathers? Scales? Wings? _____

What language does it speak? _____

What time of the day can people see this creature? _____

MYTHICAL CRISS-CROSS

Fill in this grid using the words below. Use the number of letters in each word to determine where each word fits. We did one to get you started.

L E P R E C H A U N

Word List

3 letters	5 letters	6 letters	7 letters	10 letters
ELF	FAIRY	DRAGON	BROWNIE	HIPPOGRIFF
ROC	GENIE	GOBLIN	CENTAUR	~~LEPRECHAUN~~
	GIANT	HOBBIT	GREMLIN	
4 letters	GNOME	KOBOLD	GRIFFIN	
OGRE	PIXIE	SPRITE	MERMAID	
	TROLL	WIZARD	PEGASUS	
			SANDMAN	
			UNICORN	

BIGFOOT'S COMING!

This Hidden Pictures comic has hidden objects in every panel. Can you find the CRESCENT MOON, LOLLIPOP, BROCCOLI, NEEDLE, ARTIST'S BRUSH, DRINKING STRAW, SAUCEPAN, CANOE, PEANUT, and ROLLING PIN?

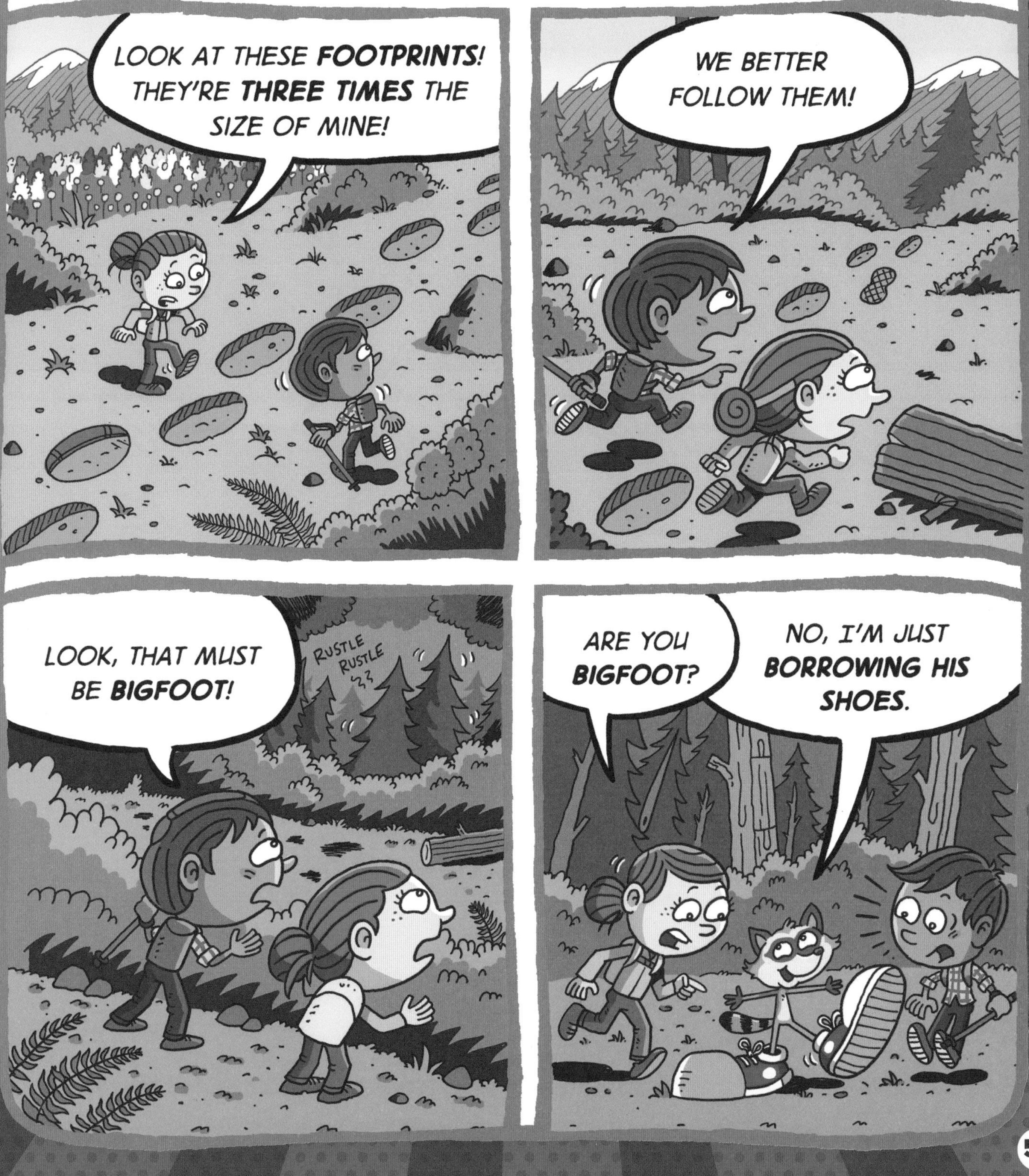
LOOK AT THESE **FOOTPRINTS!** THEY'RE **THREE TIMES** THE SIZE OF MINE!
WE BETTER FOLLOW THEM!
LOOK, THAT MUST BE **BIGFOOT!**
RUSTLE RUSTLE
ARE YOU **BIGFOOT?**
NO, I'M JUST **BORROWING HIS SHOES.**

DRAW A UNICORN

Follow the steps to draw a unicorn.

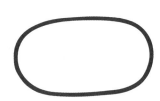

What does a unicorn call its father?

Pop-corn

COMIC CREATOR

Draw your own comic below. Try adding the motion lines you've practiced to help your characters and objects move!

THE COMIC PAGES

The speech balloons are missing in these cartoons. Can you figure out which sticker belongs with which cartoon?

1

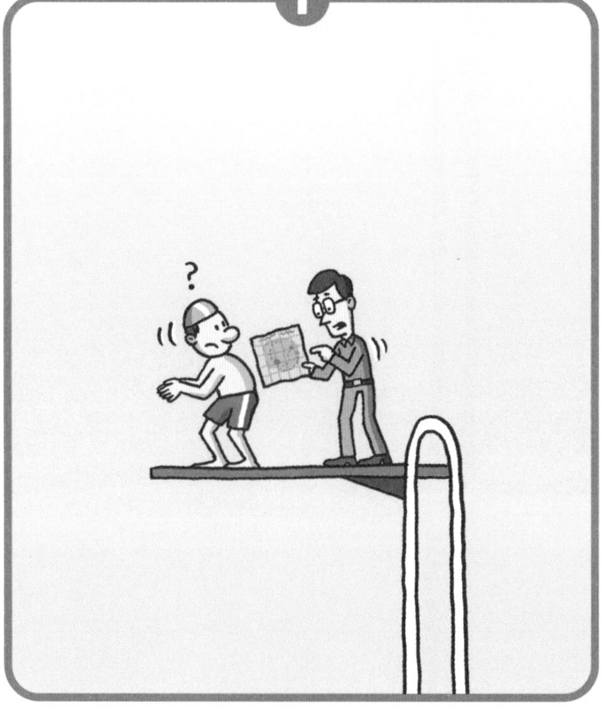

?

2

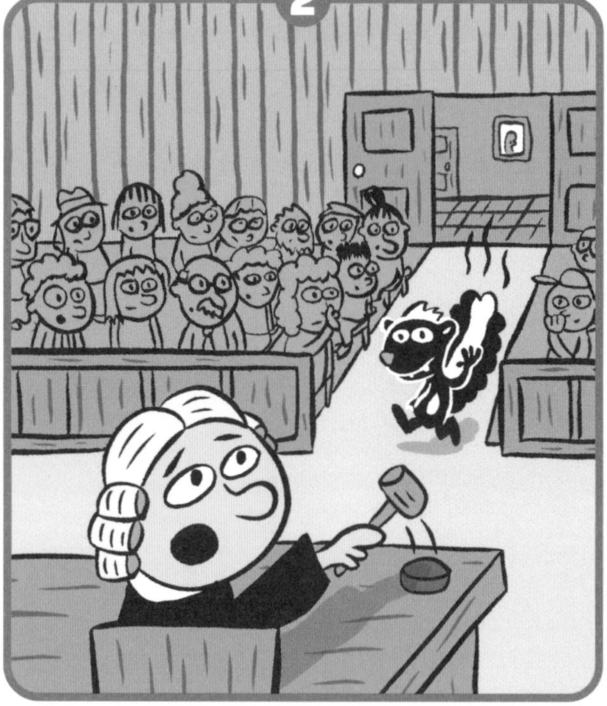

5

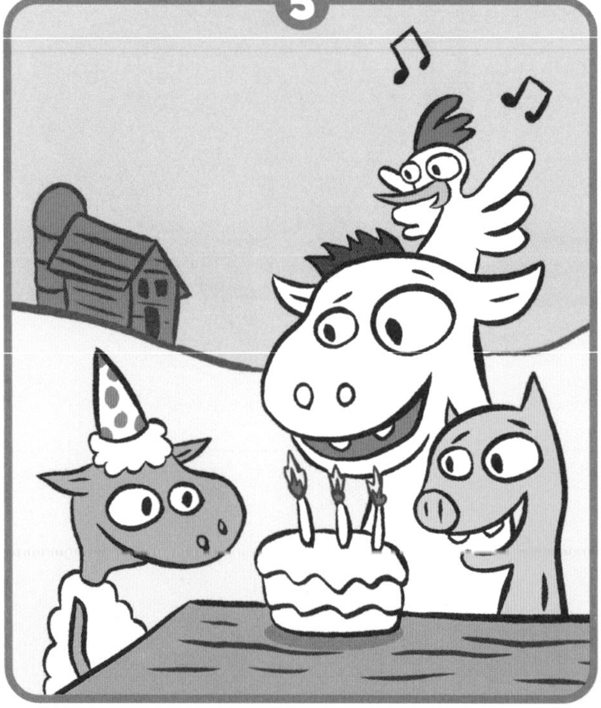

6

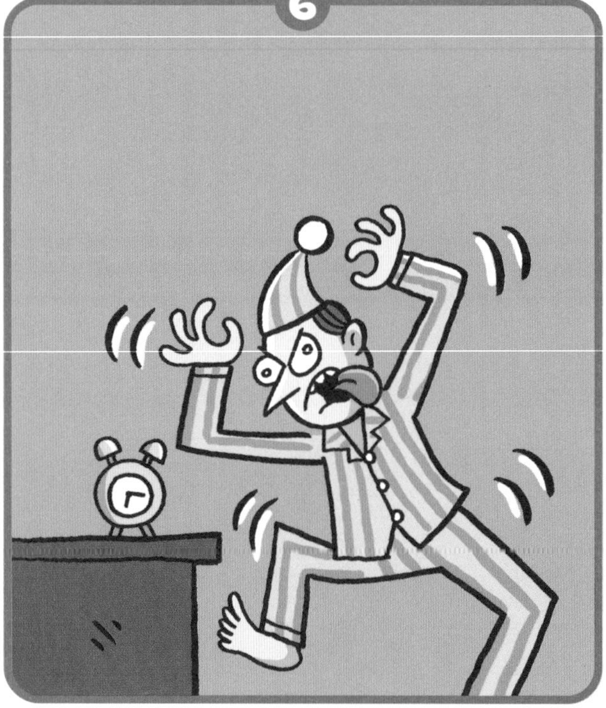

3

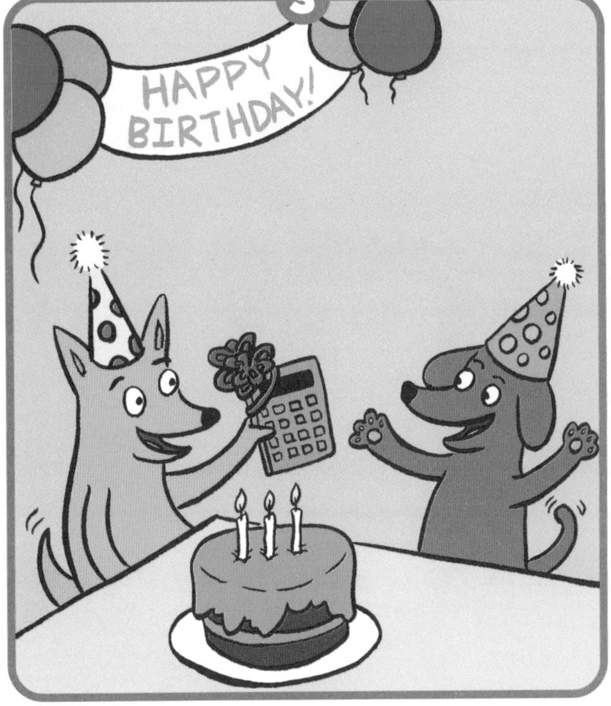
HAPPY BIRTHDAY!

4

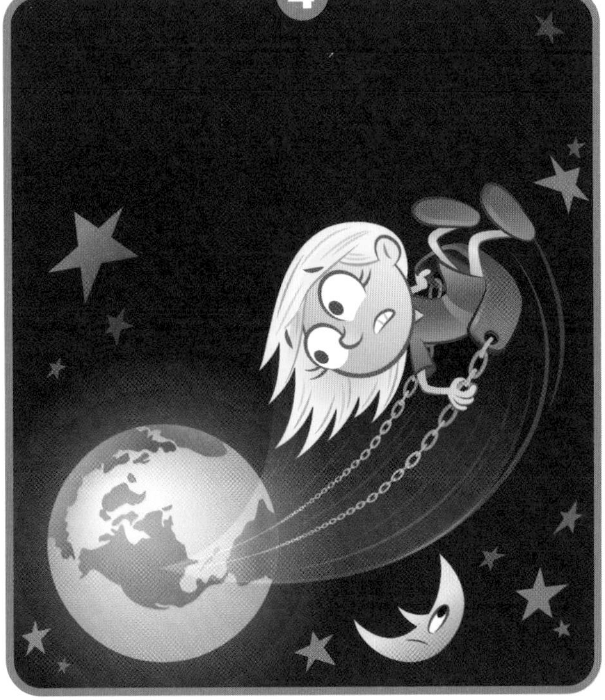

7

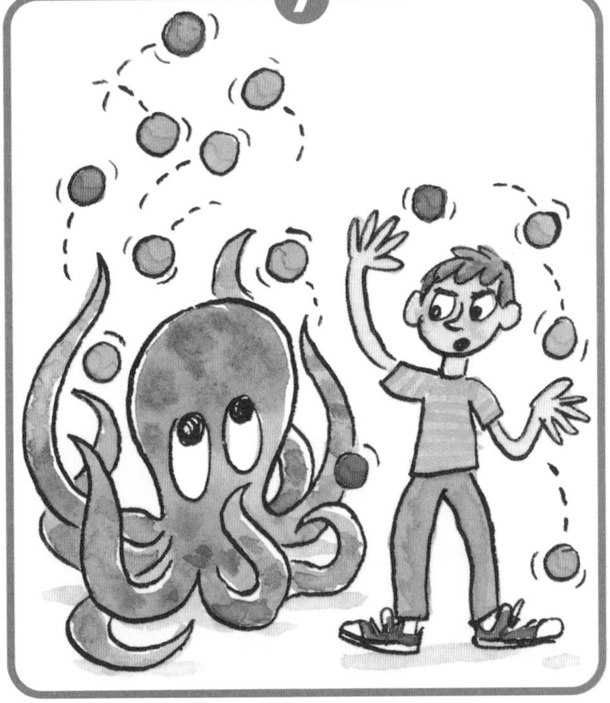

8

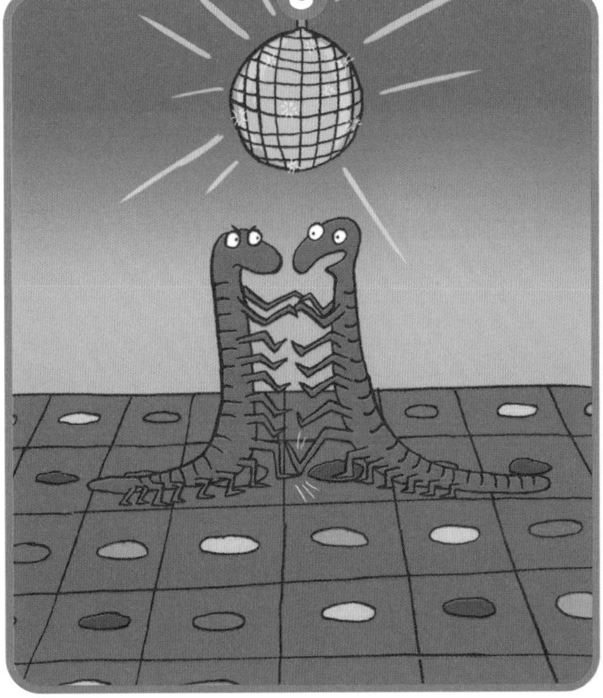

A-MAZE-ING SPACE MISSION

Soar from START (at the right) to begin the story. Find the correct path that will tell you what really happens, and then it will lead you to the next part of the story. Keep following the story maze until you reach FINISH and see what happens to Kepler, Halley, and Odyssey!

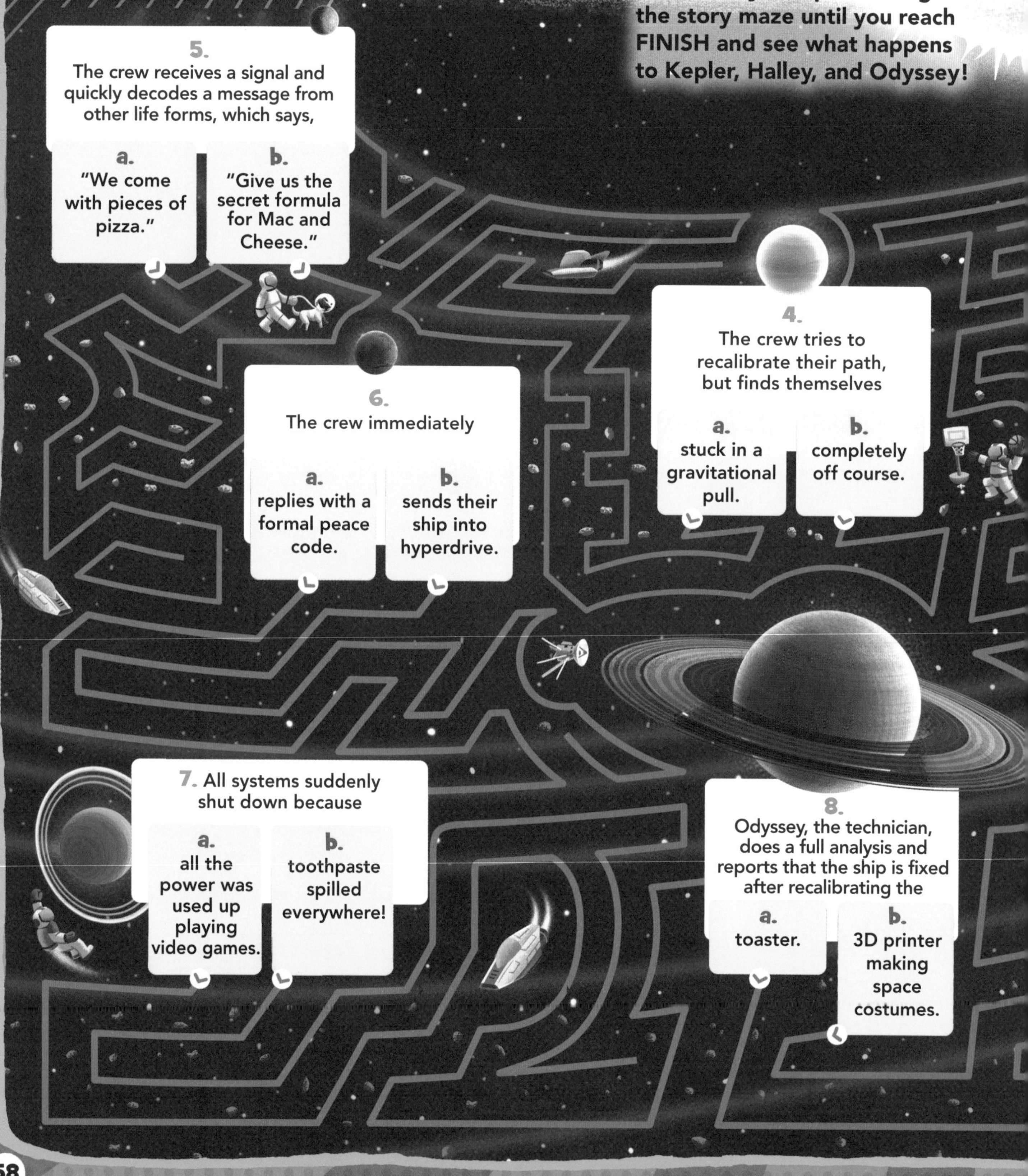

5. The crew receives a signal and quickly decodes a message from other life forms, which says,
a. "We come with pieces of pizza."
b. "Give us the secret formula for Mac and Cheese."
6. The crew immediately
a. replies with a formal peace code.
b. sends their ship into hyperdrive.
4. The crew tries to recalibrate their path, but finds themselves
a. stuck in a gravitational pull.
b. completely off course.
7. All systems suddenly shut down because
a. all the power was used up playing video games.
b. toothpaste spilled everywhere!
8. Odyssey, the technician, does a full analysis and reports that the ship is fixed after recalibrating the
a. toaster.
b. 3D printer making space costumes.

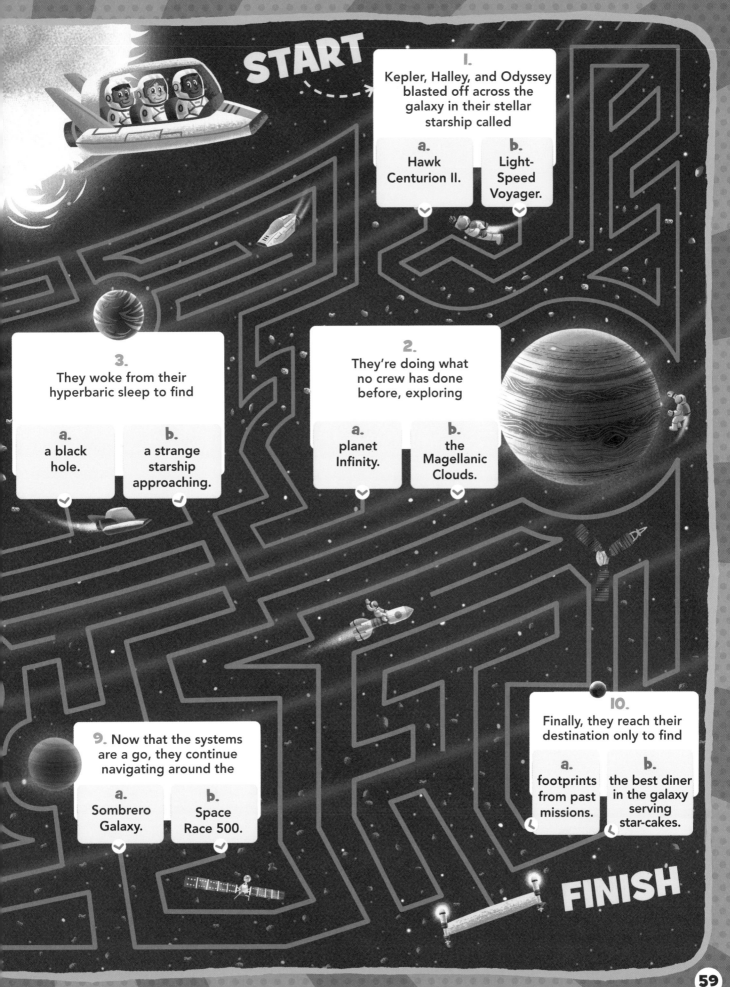

START

I.
Kepler, Halley, and Odyssey blasted off across the galaxy in their stellar starship called

a.
Hawk Centurion II.

b.
Light-Speed Voyager.

3.
They woke from their hyperbaric sleep to find

a.
a black hole.

b.
a strange starship approaching.

2.
They're doing what no crew has done before, exploring

a.
planet Infinity.

b.
the Magellanic Clouds.

9. Now that the systems are a go, they continue navigating around the

a.
Sombrero Galaxy.

b.
Space Race 500.

10.
Finally, they reach their destination only to find

a.
footprints from past missions.

b.
the best diner in the galaxy serving star-cakes.

FINISH

59

SPACE DOODLES

Use all the space on these pages to add your own outer space creations. Don't forget to use your stickers!

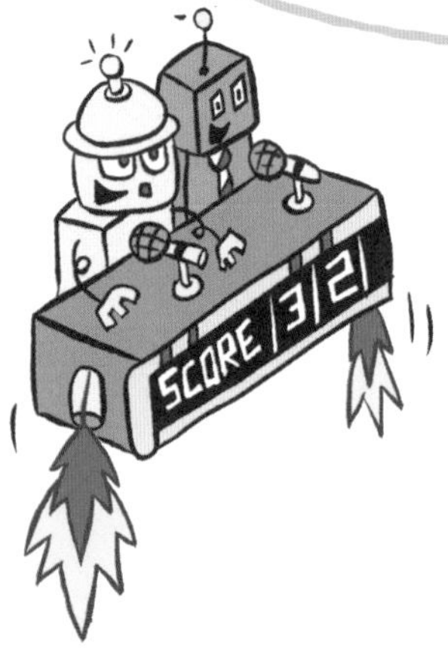
SCORE 3 21

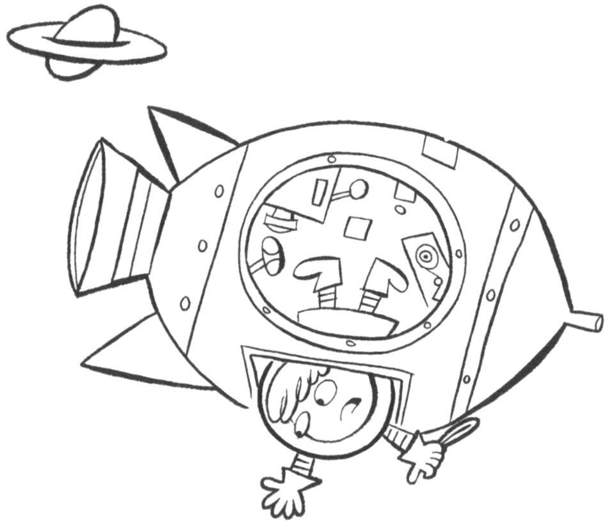

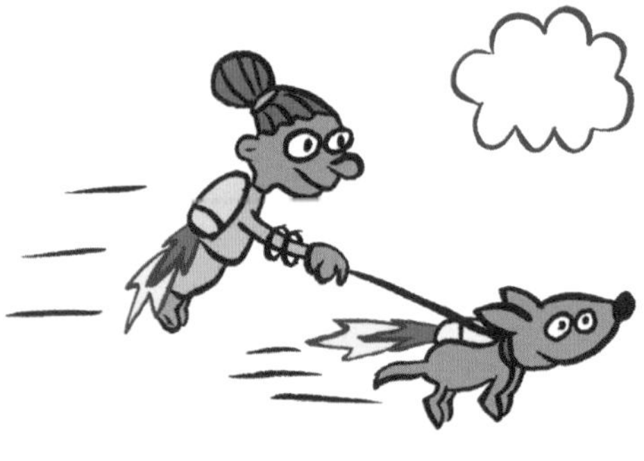

GEARED-UP MAZE

Find your way through the robot from START to FINISH.

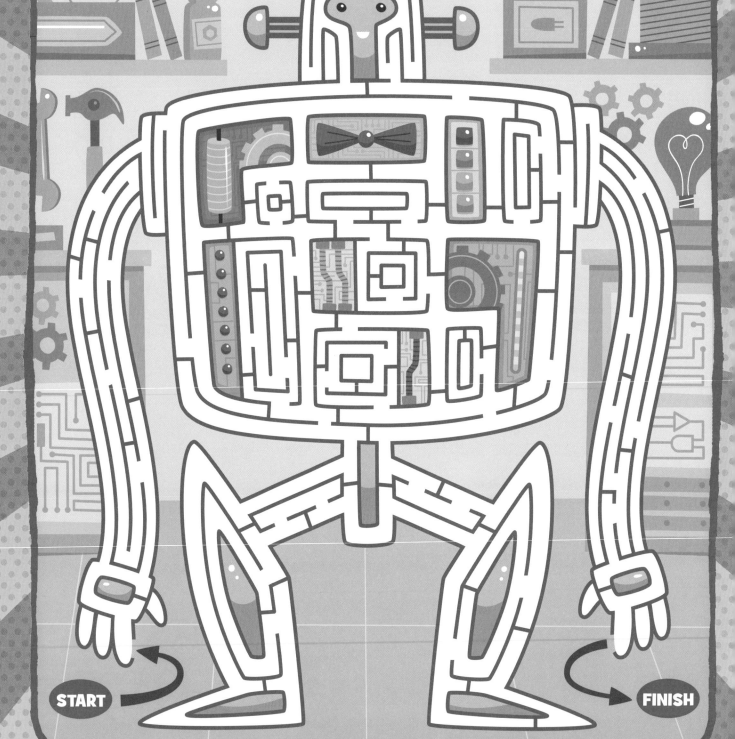

START

FINISH

JUST SAYIN'

Give this robot something to say. Then find the hidden CANOE, FLASHLIGHT, PLIERS, SCREW, and SCREWDRIVER.

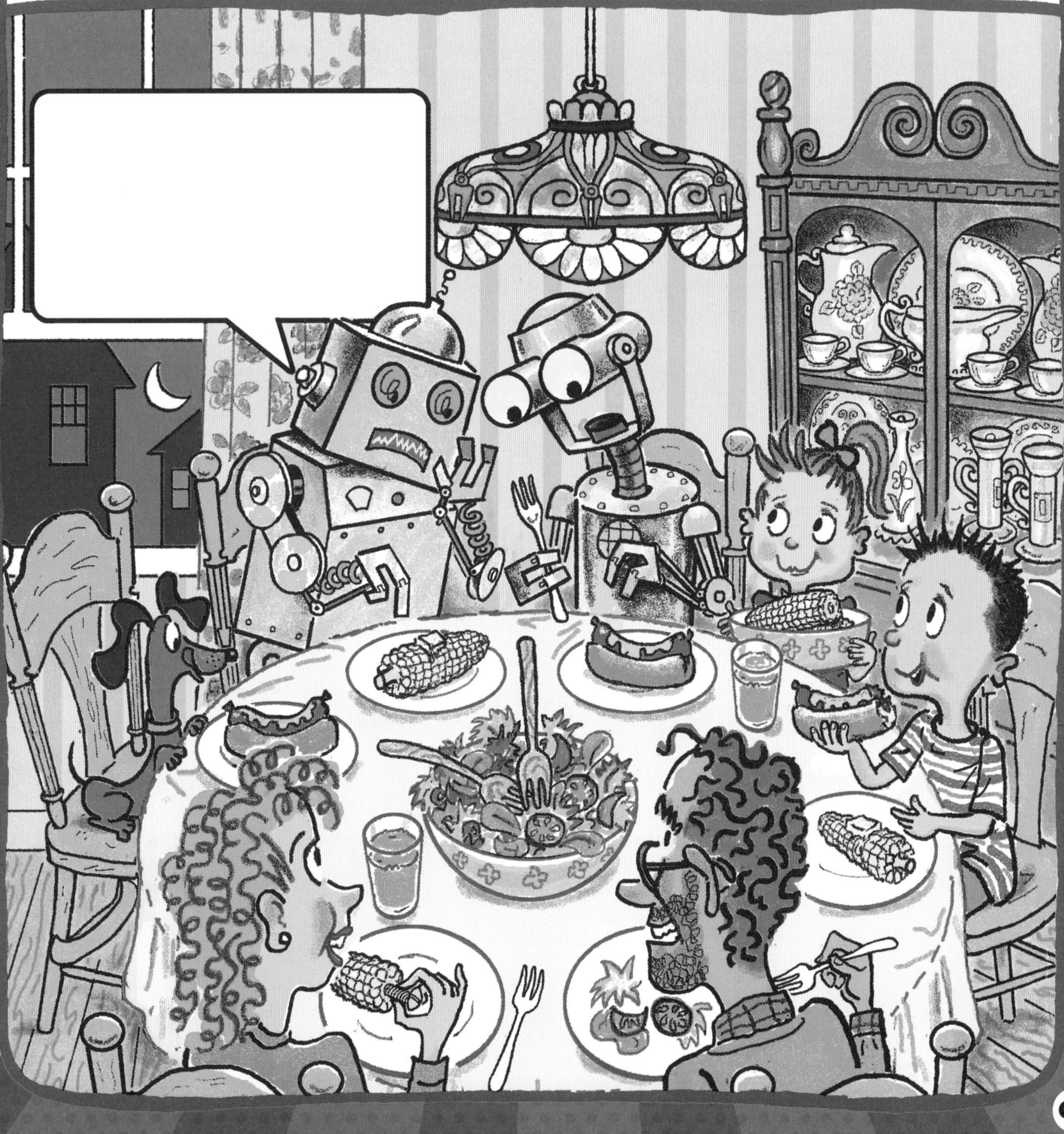

DRAW A ROBOT

Follow these steps to draw a robot.

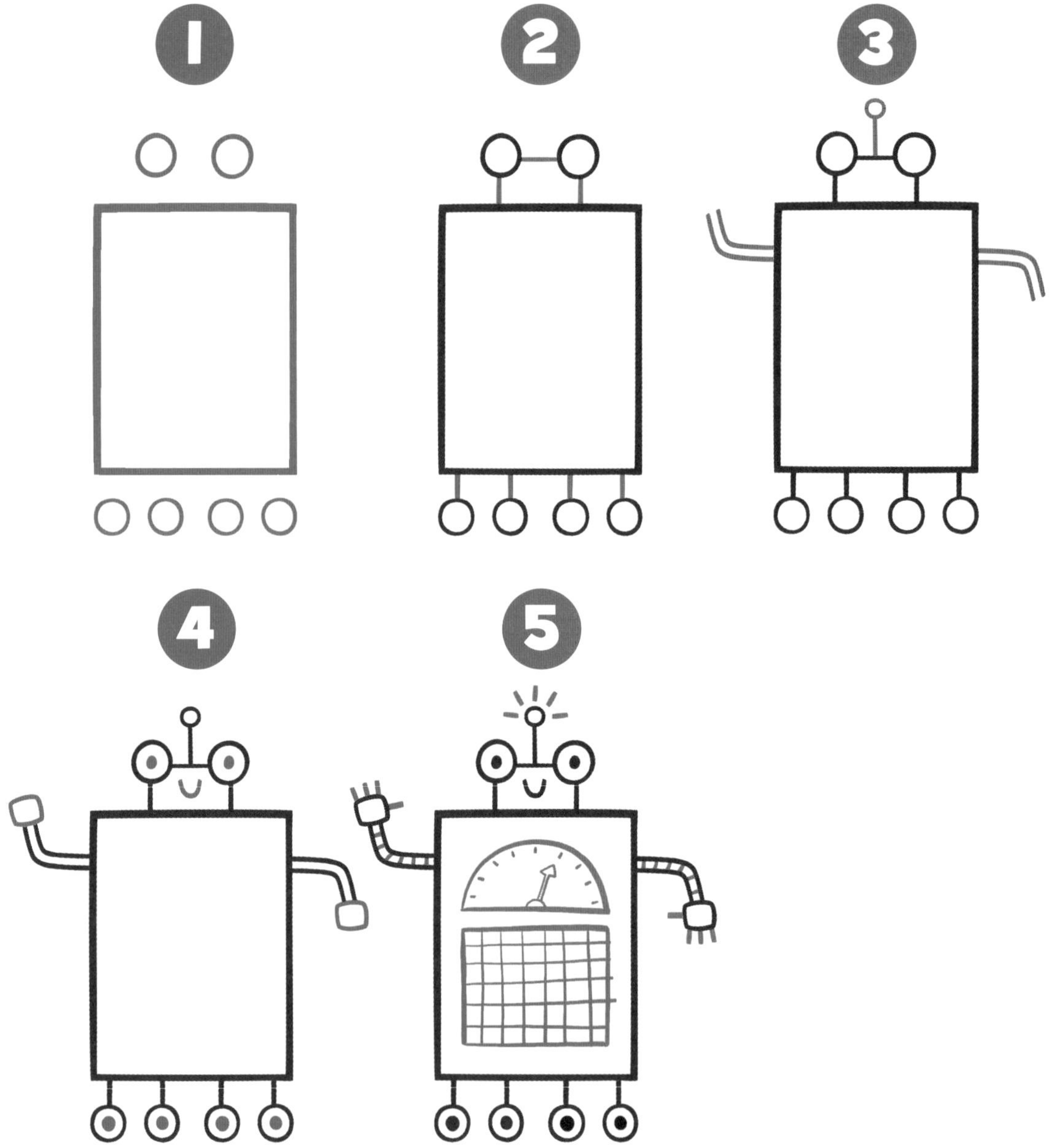
1
2
3
4
5

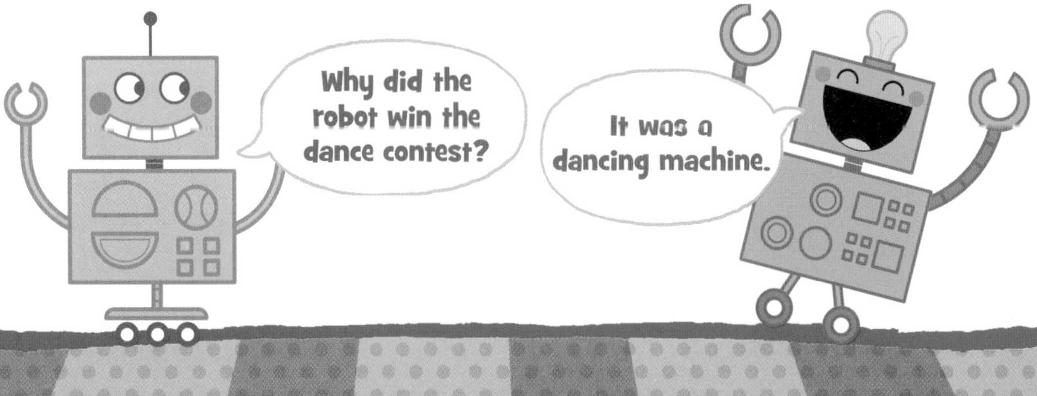
Why did the robot win the dance contest?
It was a dancing machine.

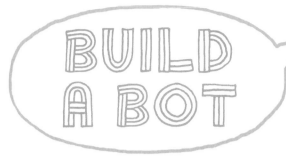

BUILD A BOT

Use your stickers to build some robots. Then use the sticker captions to give them something to say.

JUST SAYIN'

Give this student something to say. Then find the hidden BANANA, CELL PHONE, ELEPHANT, PENCIL, and TOASTER.

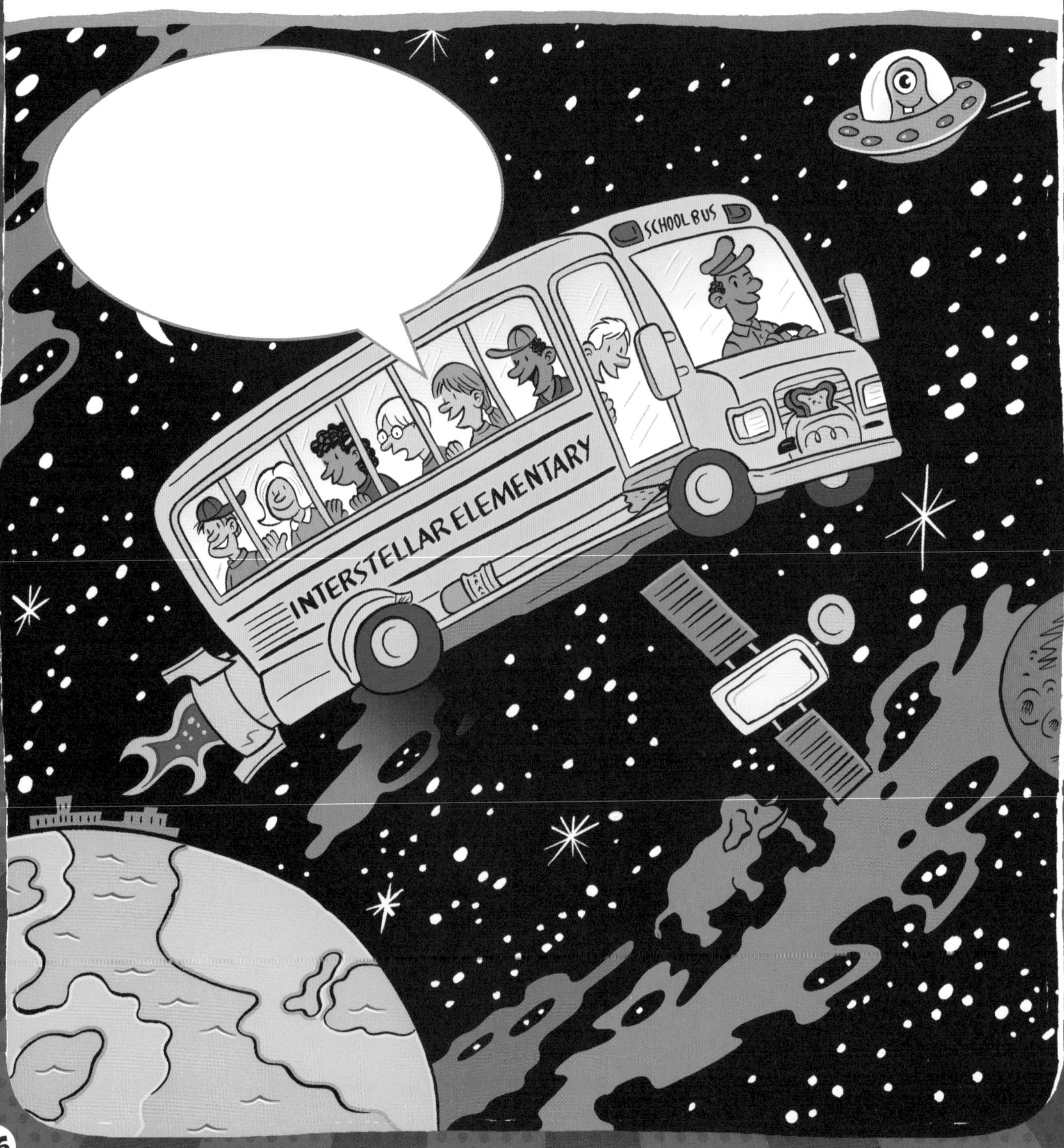
SCHOOL BUS
INTERSTELLAR ELEMENTARY

SPACE CODE

Use the code to fill in the spaces below and finish the jokes.

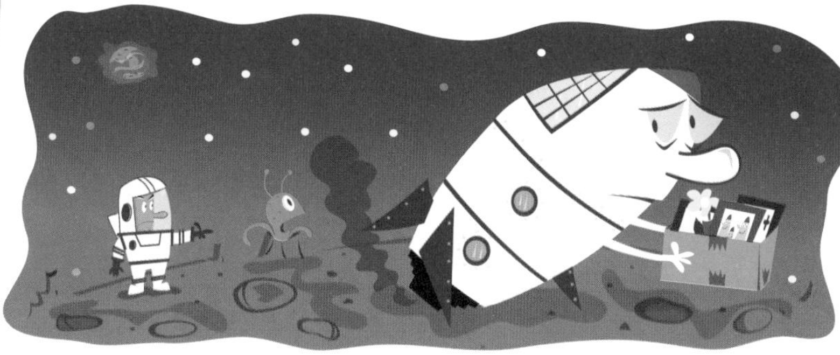

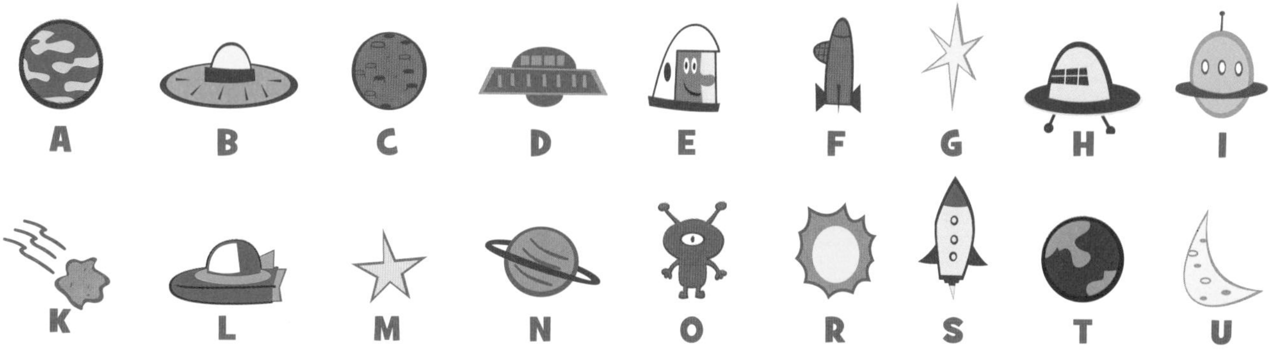
A
B
C
D
E
F
G
H
I
K
L
M
N
O
R
S
T
U

How did the rocket lose its job?

___ ___ ___ ___ ___ ___ ___ ___ ___ ___.

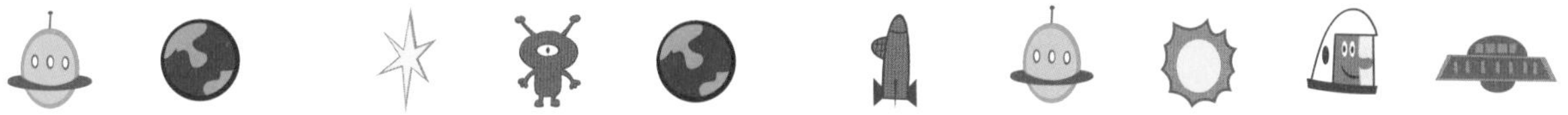

What meal do astronauts like best?

___ ___ ___ ___ ___ ___

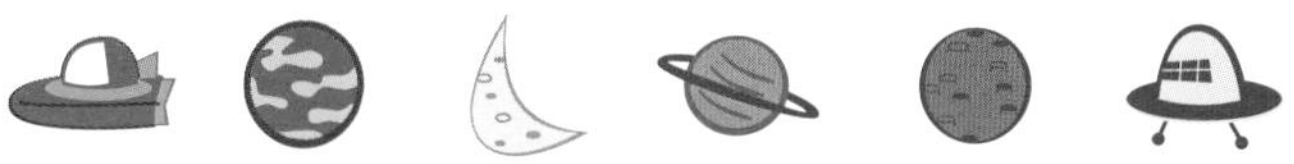

What do young astronauts like to read?

___ ___ ___ ___ ___ ___ ___ ___ ___ ___

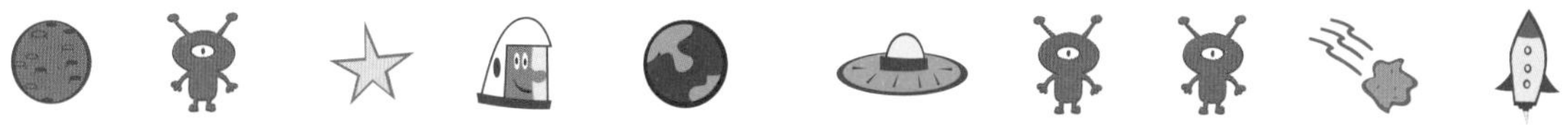

DRAW AN ALIEN

Follow the steps to draw an alien.

1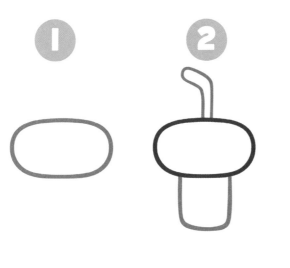

2

3

4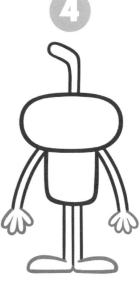

5

How do aliens count to 27?

On their fingers.

COMIC CREATOR

Use this space to create your own outer space comic. Will it be out of this world?

THE COMIC PAGES

The speech balloons are missing in these cartoons. Can you figure out which sticker belongs with which cartoon?

1

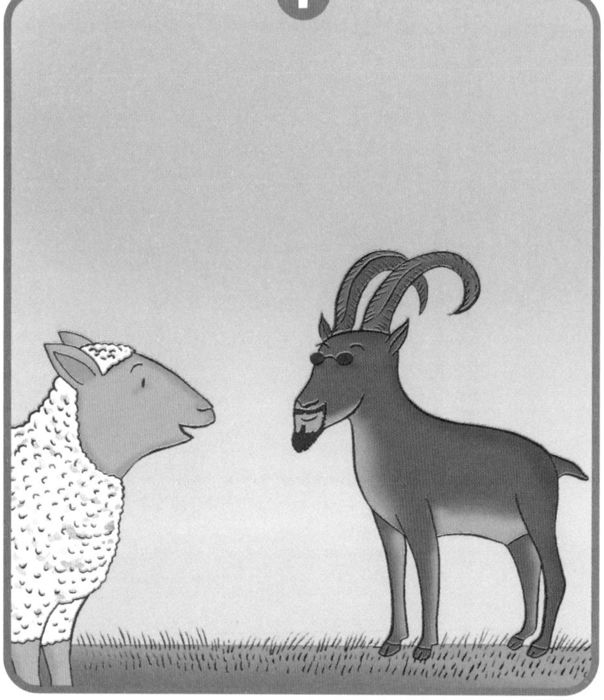

2

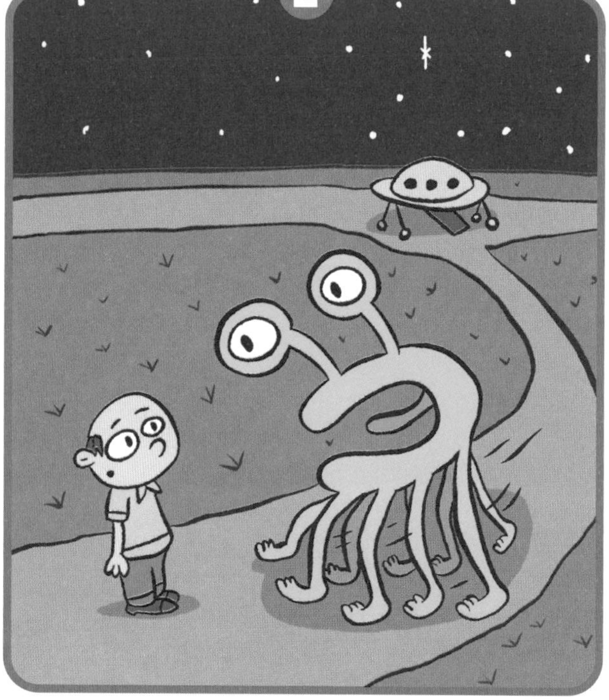

5

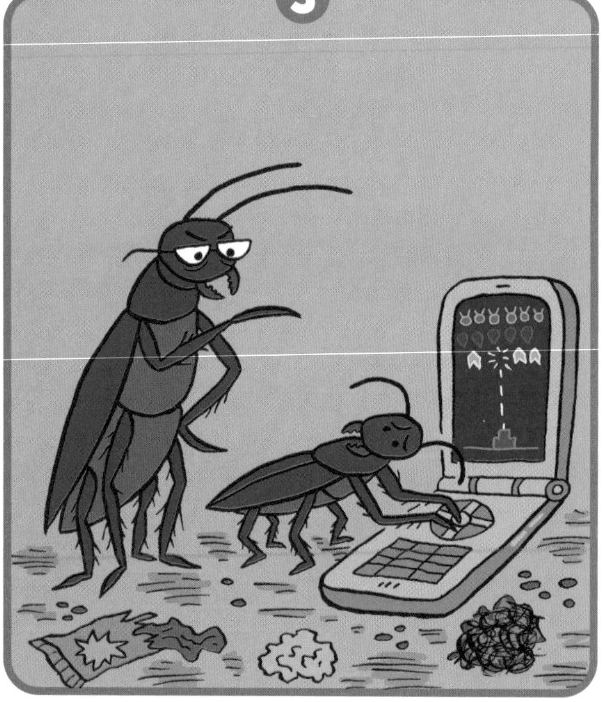

6

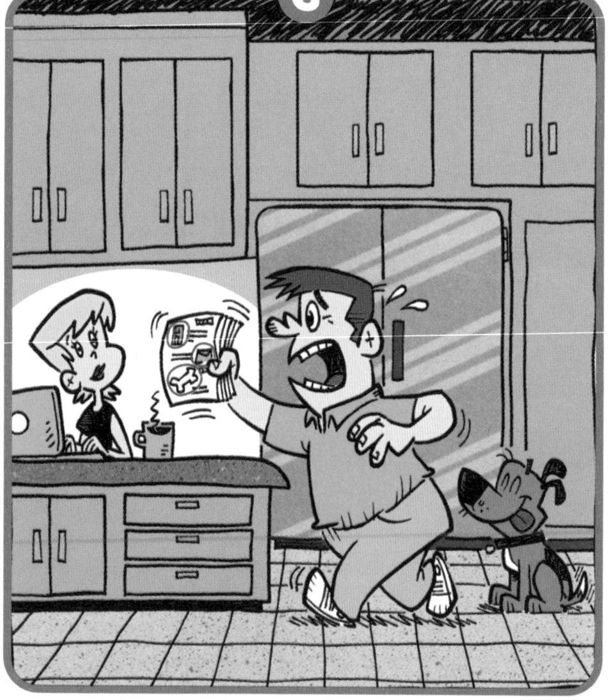

3

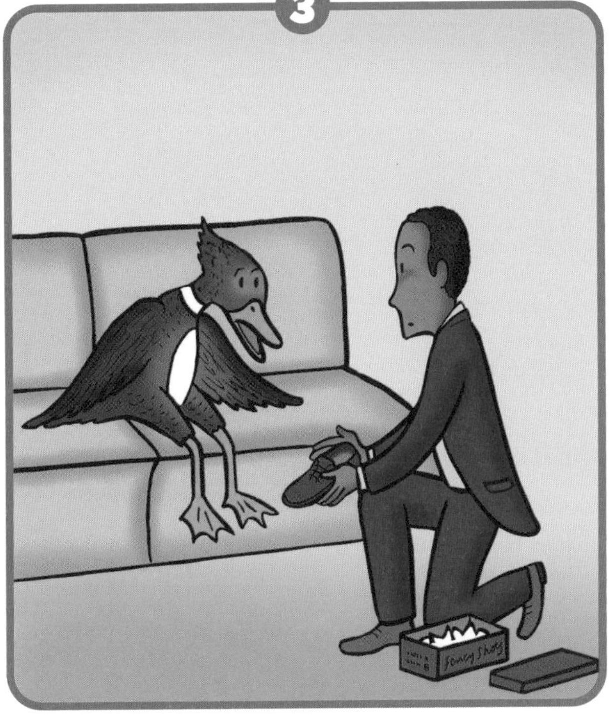

4

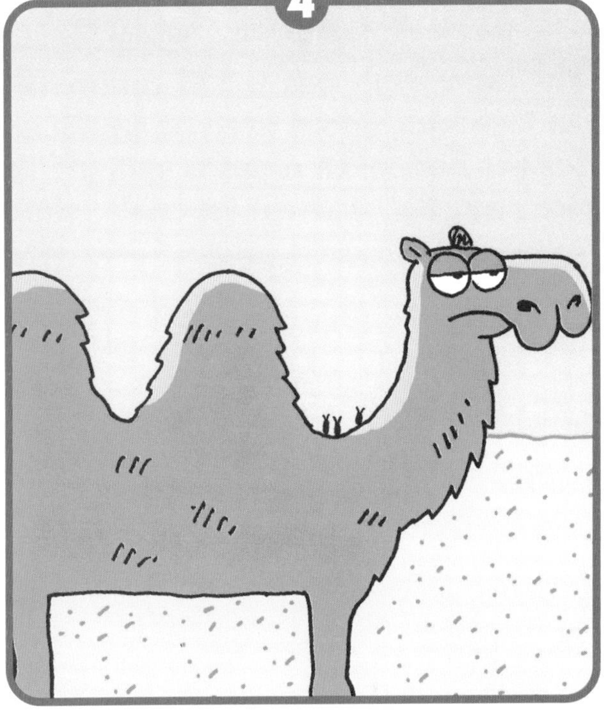

7

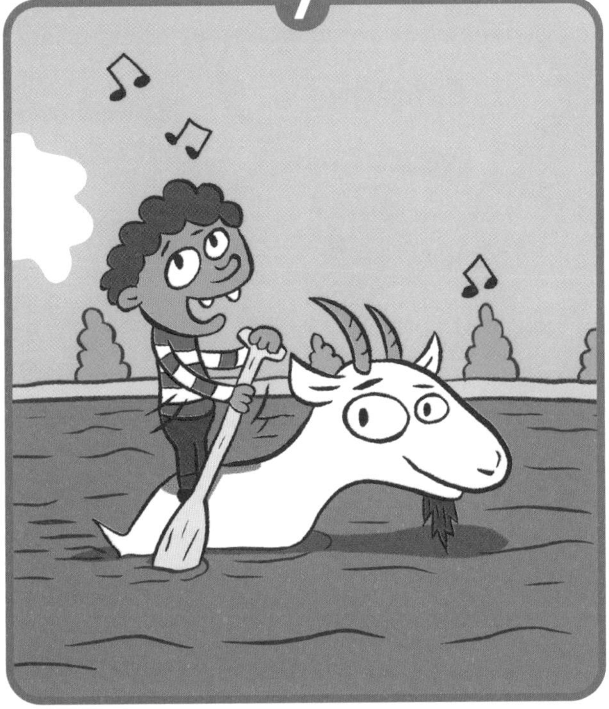

8

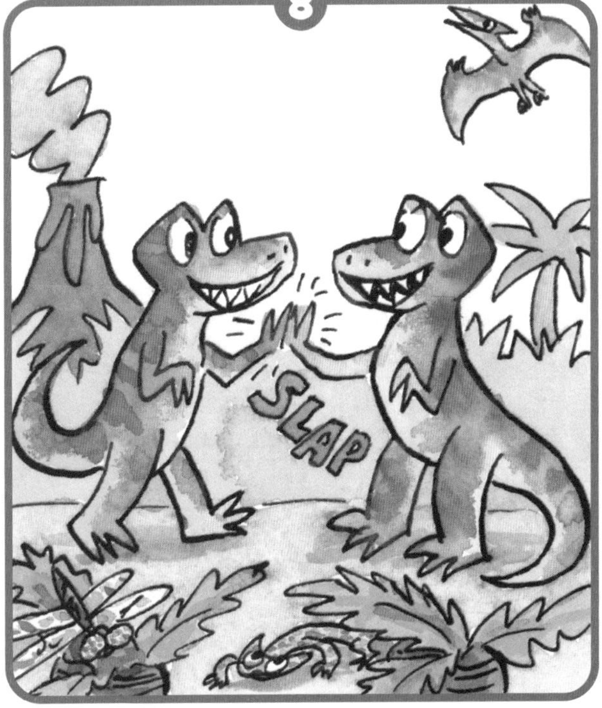
SLAP

Finish the Comic

The Pepper Caper

The countertop was full of commotion when Inspector Spoon arrived on the scene. Pepper had taken a nasty spill off the spice rack. Salt seemed especially shaken.

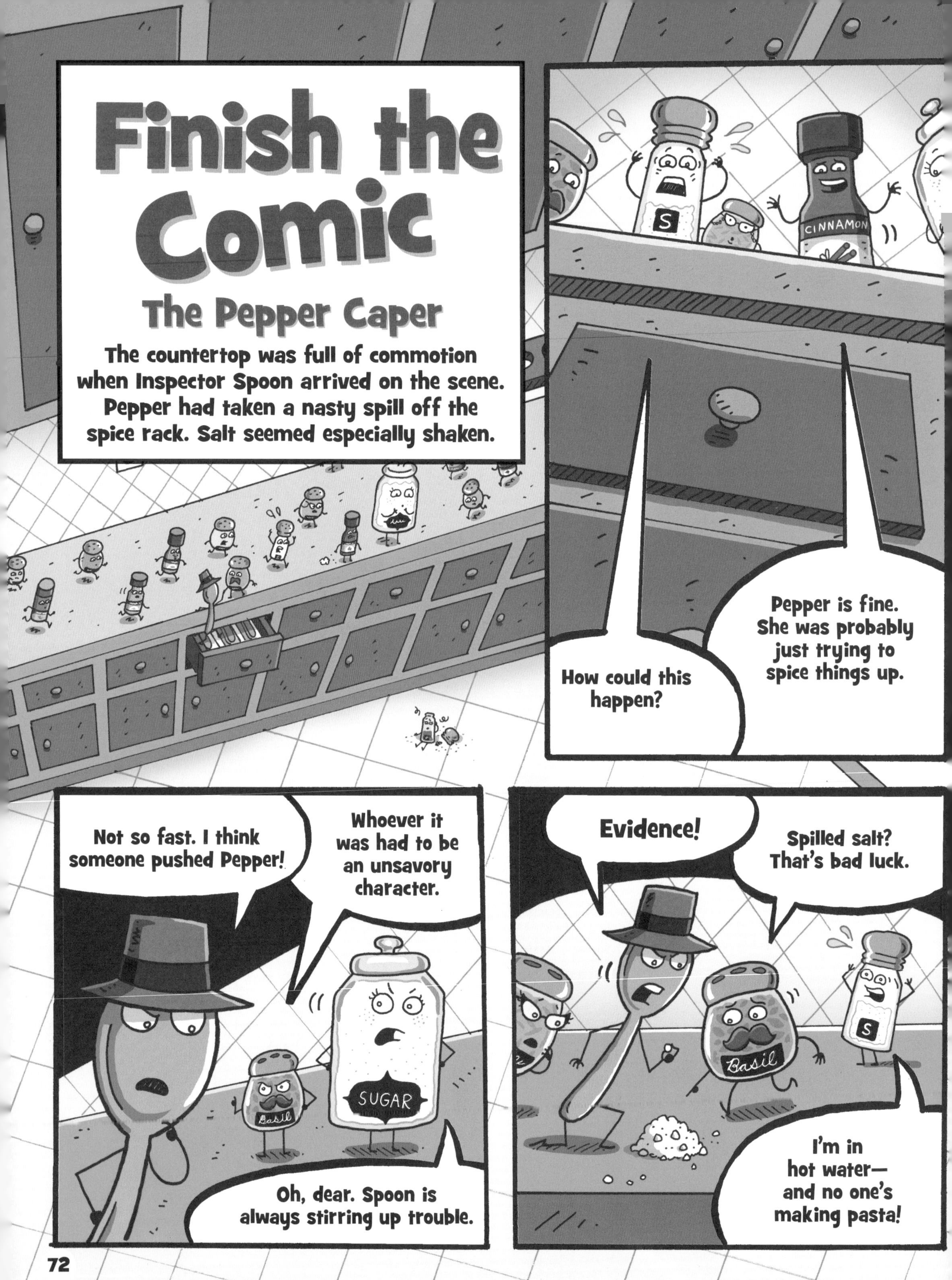
S
CINNAMON
How could this happen?
Pepper is fine. She was probably just trying to spice things up.
Not so fast. I think someone pushed Pepper!
Whoever it was had to be an unsavory character.
SUGAR
Basil
Oh, dear. Spoon is always stirring up trouble.
Evidence!
Spilled salt? That's bad luck.
Basil
S
I'm in hot water— and no one's making pasta!

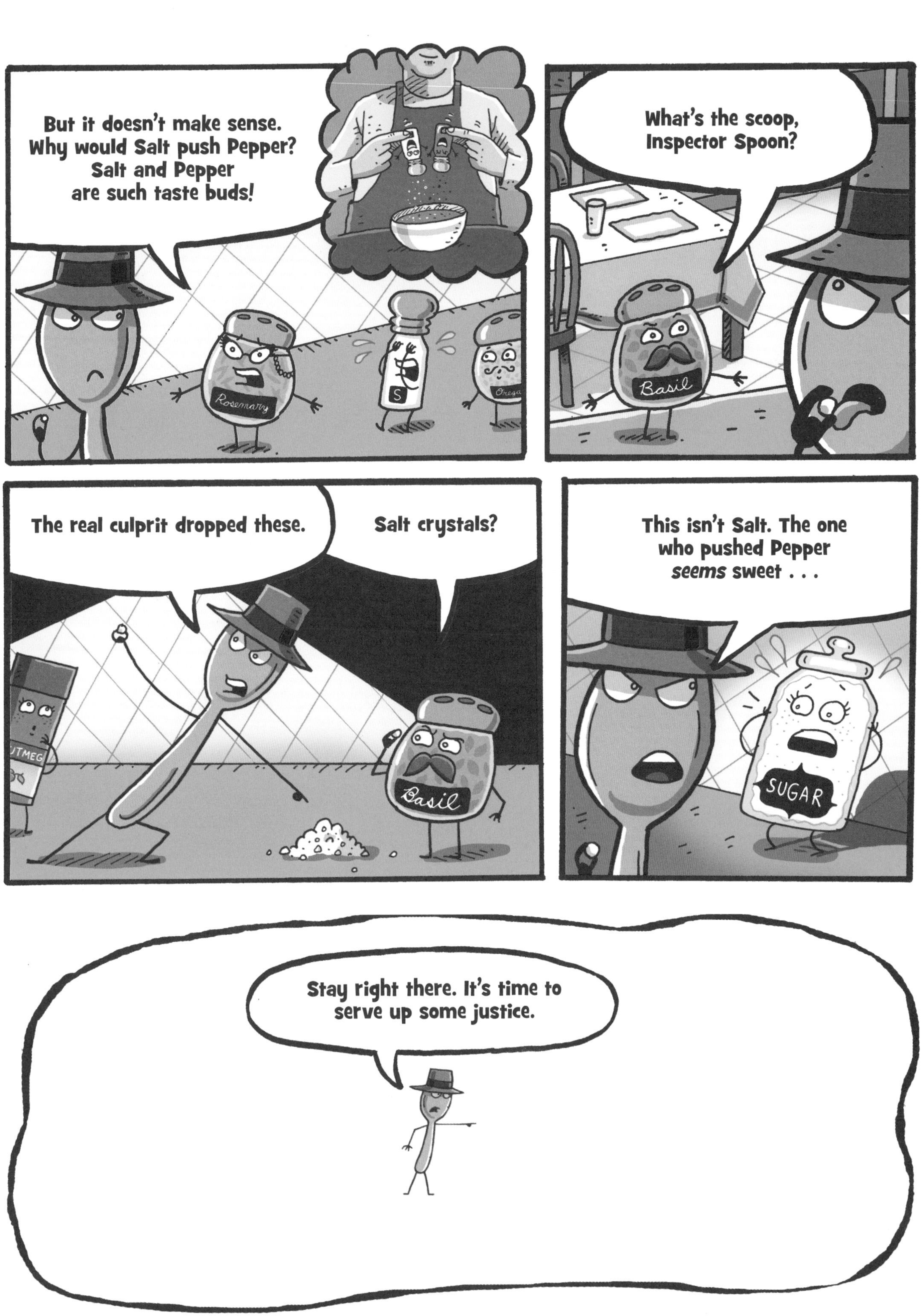
But it doesn't make sense. Why would Salt push Pepper? Salt and Pepper are such taste buds!
Rosemary
S
What's the scoop, Inspector Spoon?
Basil
The real culprit dropped these.
Salt crystals?
Basil
This isn't Salt. The one who pushed Pepper *seems* sweet . . .
SUGAR
Stay right there. It's time to serve up some justice.

Who is responsible for Pepper's tumble? Draw in who you think the culprit is.

DETECTIVE DOODLES

These detectives are following an important lead. Can you doodle a trail for them to follow? What other clues have been left behind? Don't forget to use your stickers!

SCENE OF THE RHYME

The world-famous Inspector Hink Pink has another case to solve. First, use the stickers to finish the picture. Then look for pairs of rhyming words in the scene. The inspector found a frog log. How many more can you find?

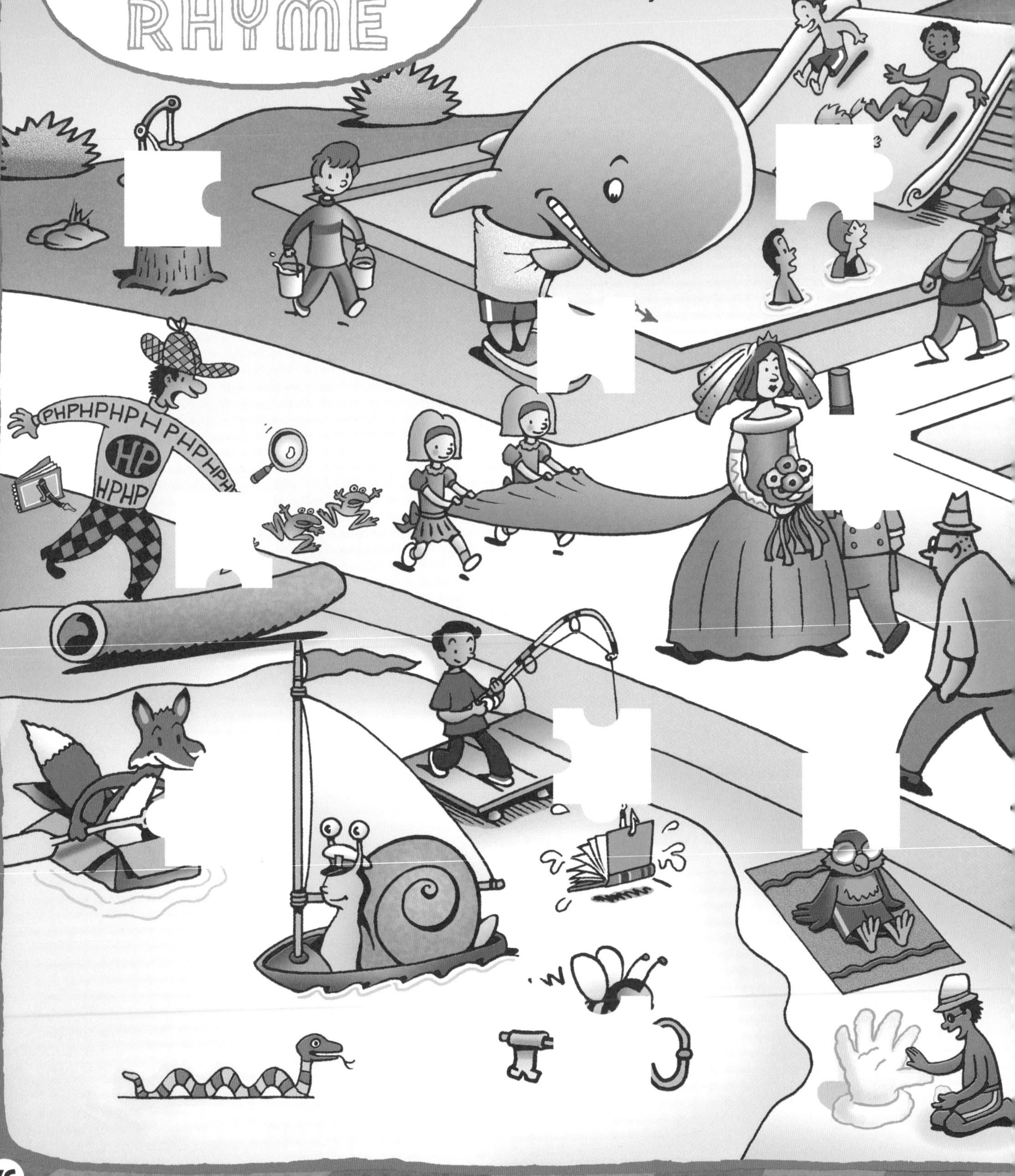
HP

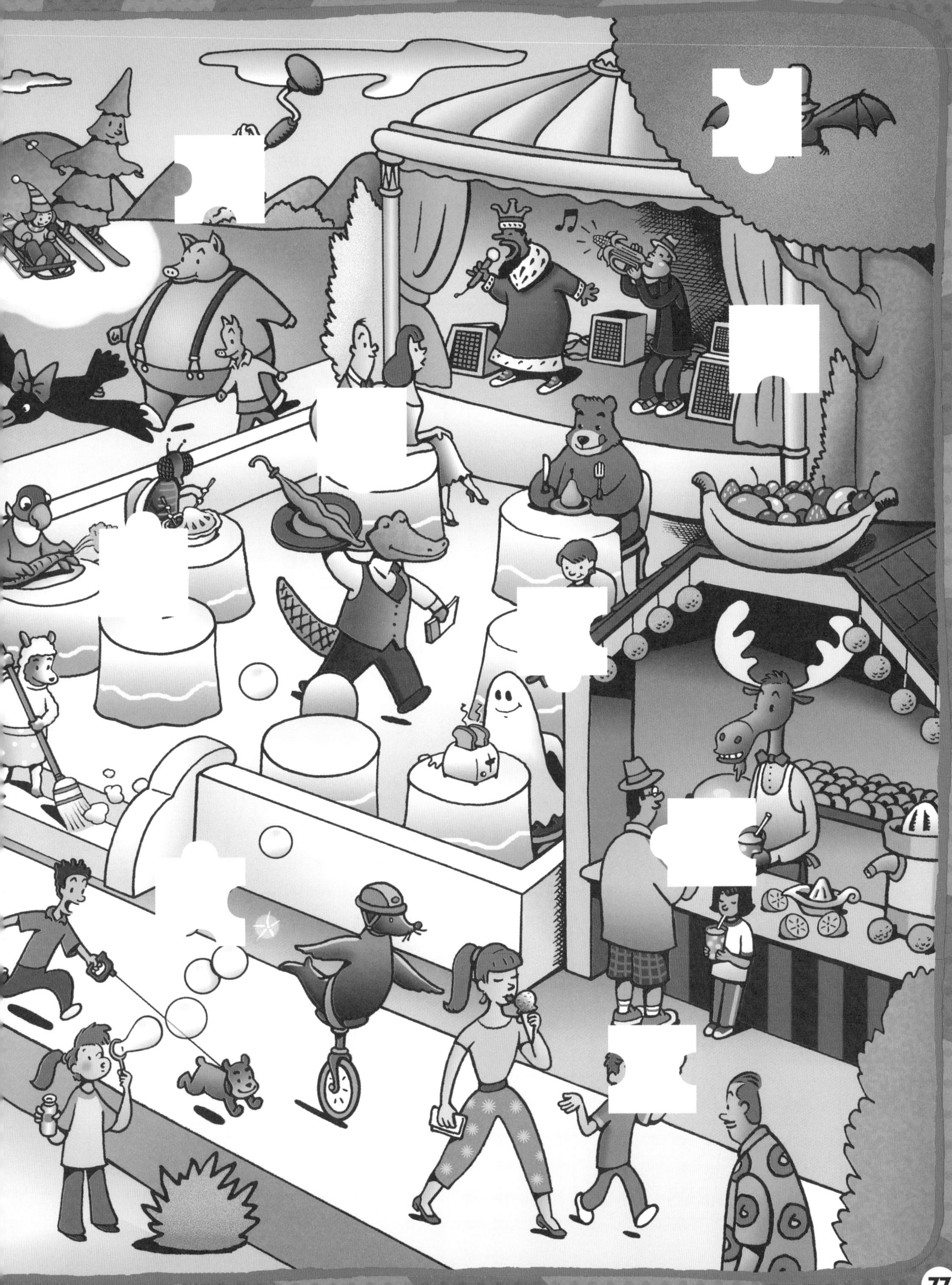

FIND THE SPIES

Calling all detectives! Ten suspects are on the loose in Puzzlemania Park! Take a good look at the posters. Then see if you can find each suspect on the next page. Each is wearing the same clothes as on the wanted posters. Can you nab them all?

WANTED

YUL B. SORRY

WANTED

MR. REE

WANTED

BEN DONNE

WANTED

LOUIS TOOTH

WANTED

ALENE MACHINE

WANTED

CONSTANCE BICKERING

WANTED

AVA LANCHE

WANTED

DELIA CARDS

WANTED

HARRY FACE

WANTED

KENT STOP

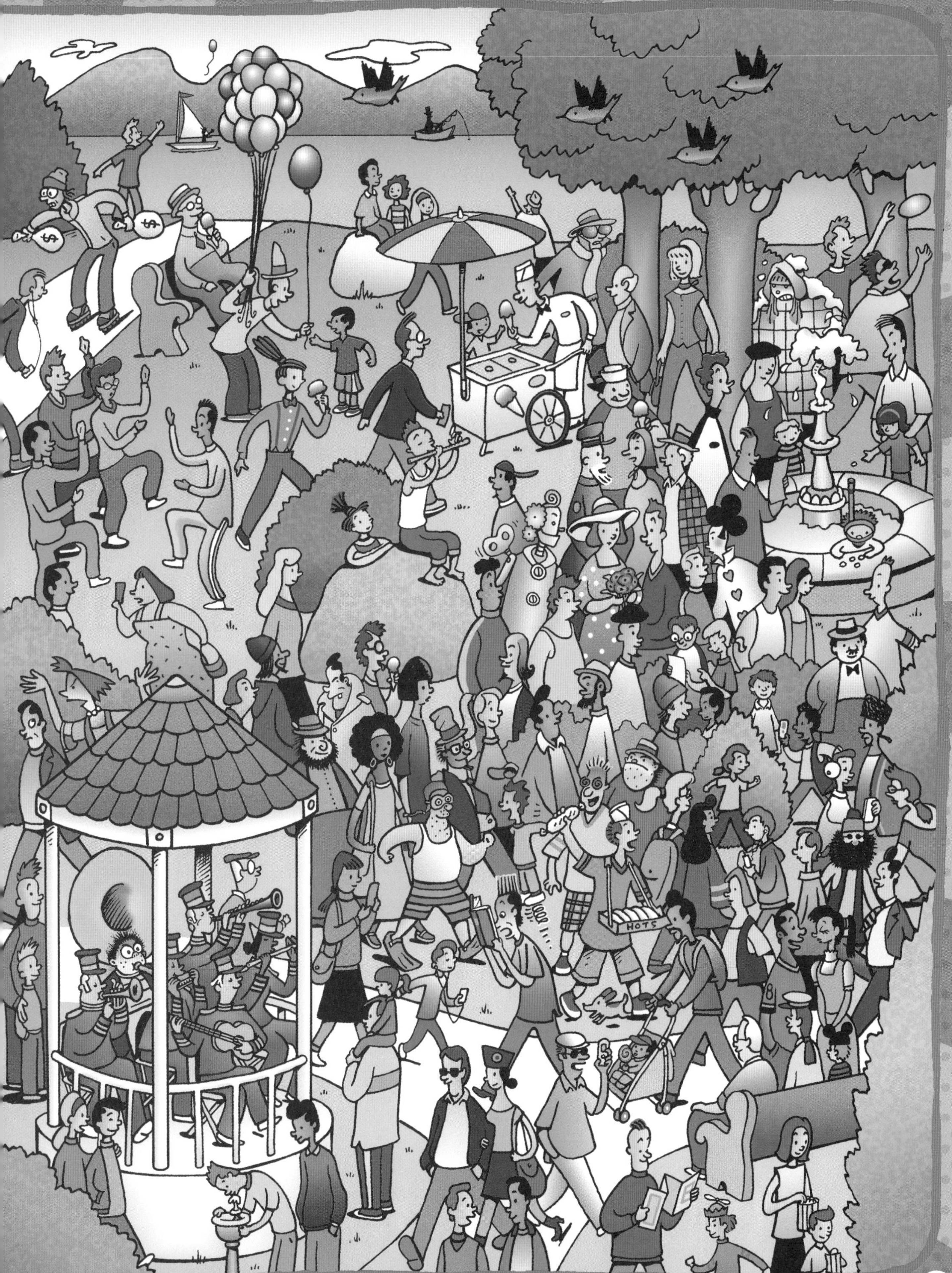
HOTS

JUST SAYIN'

Oh, no! Hammy is missing. But don't worry, Heidi and Zeke have taken the case. Give Heidi something to say. Then find the hidden TOOTHBRUSH, TACK, YO-YO, DRINKING STRAW, SLICE OF BREAD, MAGIC WAND, CRESCENT MOON, BOLT, NAIL, FISHHOOK, CRAYON, TEACUP, and MAGNET.

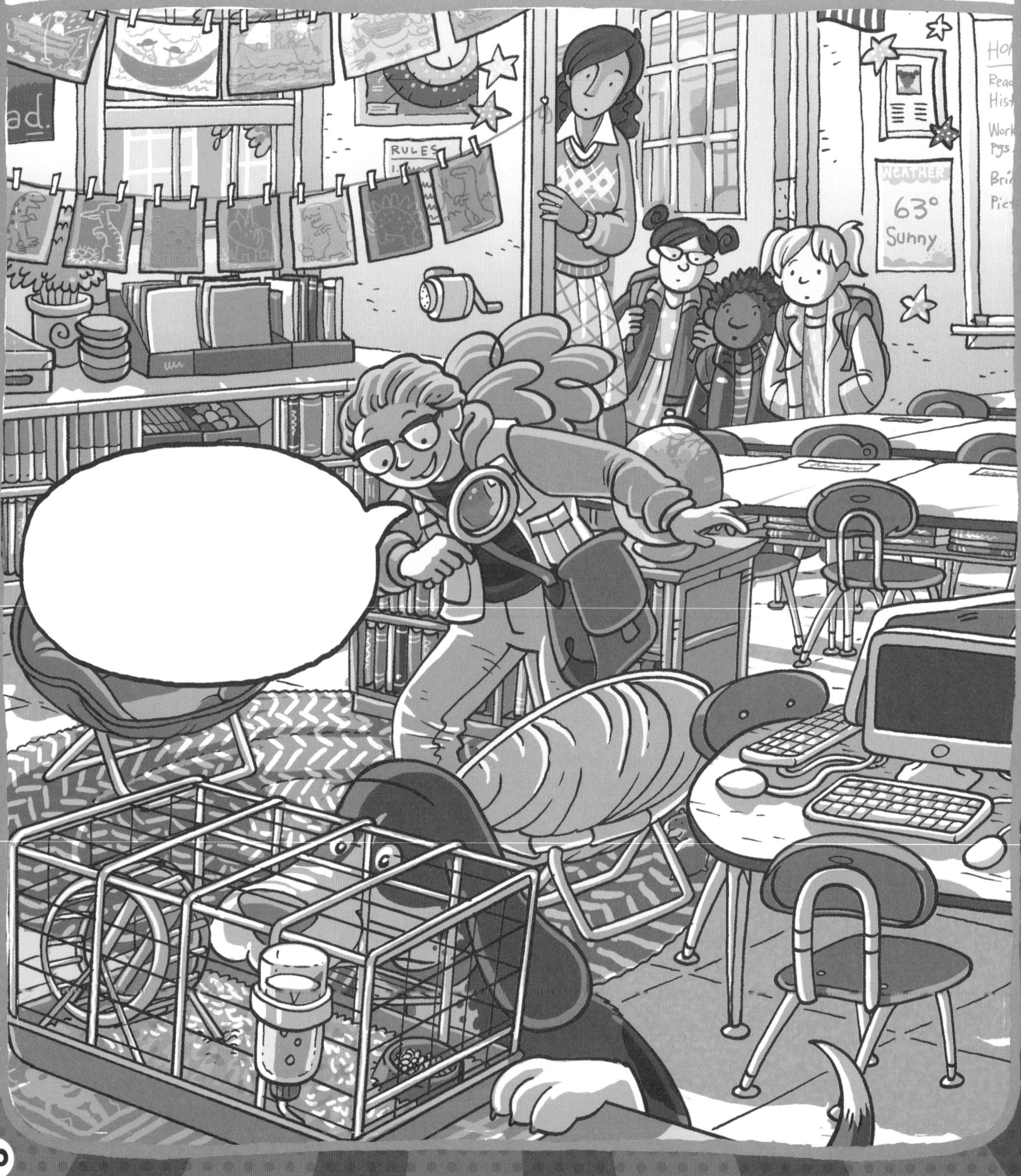
RULES
WEATHER
63°
Sunny

WHAT'S YOUR DISGUISE?

The mission is a go! But you can't disguise the fact that you're having a hard time picking out the perfect incognito getup for your next case. Take this quiz to see which undercover outfit you should choose.

1. **Which kind of music is your detective theme song?**
   a. Dramatic music, like a movie theme song.
   b. Playful, magical tunes, maybe with tinkling bells or a xylophone.
   c. A mash-up of styles, like a rap version of "Twinkle, Twinkle, Little Star" with a burst of banjo.
   d. A march with lots of drums.

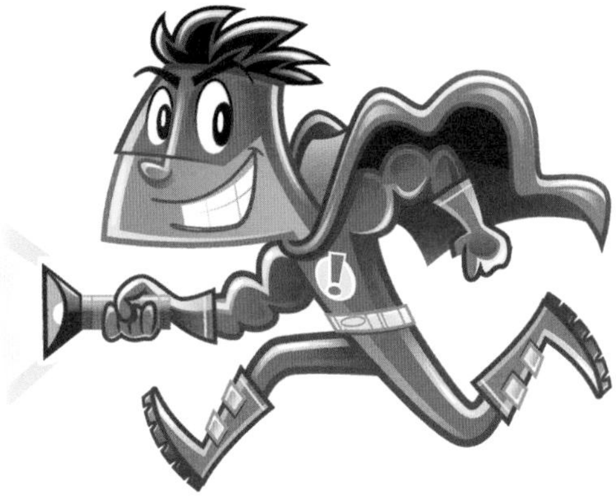

2. **Your favorite books are:**
   a. Filled with action and lots of excitement!
   b. Fantasy stories with imaginary characters.
   c. All types. There's no way to pick just one kind!
   d. About real people, animals, and cool facts.

3. **You have free time! What do you want to do?**
   a. Film mini videos of my adventures.
   b. Draw kingdoms full of creatures I made up myself.
   c. Juggle while counting in another language while standing on one foot.
   d. Look up stuff about things I'm interested in.

4. **A new movie is coming out called *Little Red Riding Hood in Space*! Will you go see it?**
   a. Sounds like an adventure. I'm in!
   b. Sure. I always like to see creative variations on classic tales.
   c. Only if there are alien wolves.
   d. Probably not. But if it were a true movie about outer space, then absolutely yes!

If you answered mostly A's, be a hero! Dress as a real hero, like a firefighter, or an imaginary one, like a comic book superhero. Who would want to mess with you?

If you answered mostly B's, use your imagination! Dress as a character from a myth or fairy tale, or invent your own creature from another world. That will really throw off the suspects.

If you answered mostly C's, mix and match! Combine a bunch of ideas into a unique disguise, like a rock-star dinosaur or a ballerina astronaut. No one will ever recognize you.

If you answered mostly D's, make it real! Deck yourself out as a historical figure. Be Cleopatra, a president, or Albert Einstein. Channel one of the greats as you build your case.

DRAW SPY GEAR

Follow the steps to draw some spy gear.

① ② ③ ④

What do detectives do when they are scared?

They go undercovers.

COMIC CREATOR

Use the blank panels to create your very own mystery comic. Who will be on the case?

SCRAMBLED SOUNDS

Something is odd about the sounds at this party. For example, the goose should be saying HONK instead of KOHN. Can you unscramble the other sound words below? For hints, find the words in the scene.

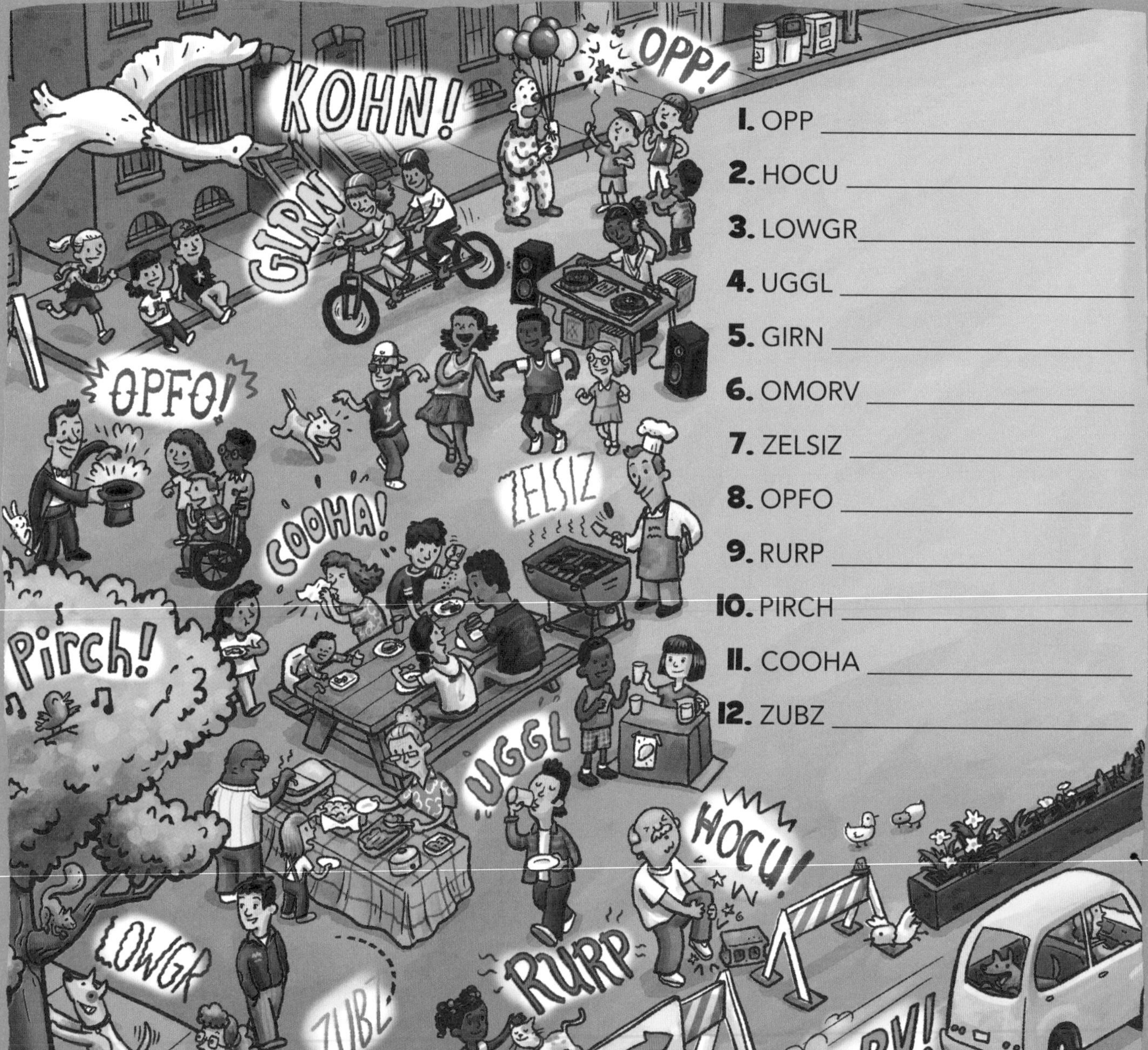

KOHN!
OPP!
GIRN
OPFO!
ZELSIZ
COOHA!
Pirch!
UGGL
HOCU!
LOWGR
RURP
ZUBZ
OMORV!

1. OPP ____________________
2. HOCU ____________________
3. LOWGR ____________________
4. UGGL ____________________
5. GIRN ____________________
6. OMORV ____________________
7. ZELSIZ ____________________
8. OPFO ____________________
9. RURP ____________________
10. PIRCH ____________________
11. COOHA ____________________
12. ZUBZ ____________________

CAPTION THIS!

Give each of these comics a silly caption.

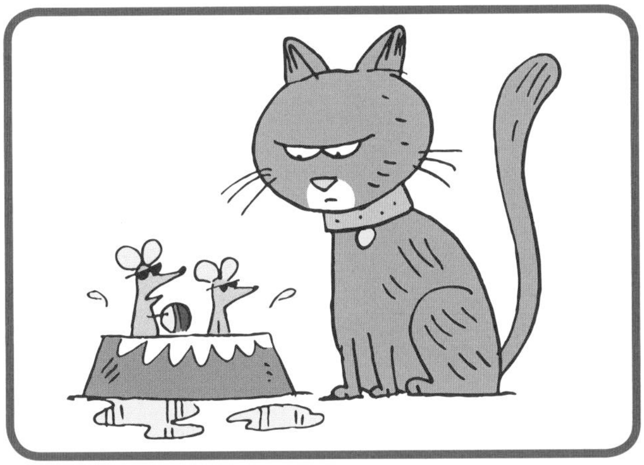

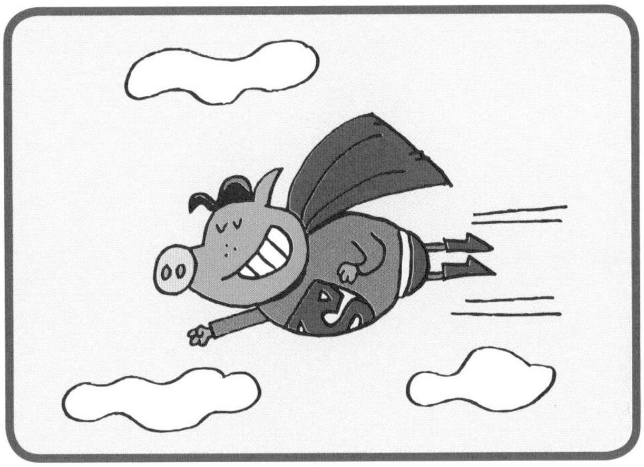

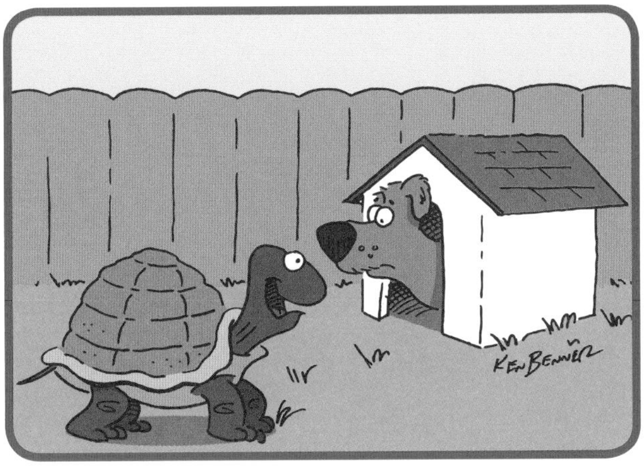
KEN BENNER

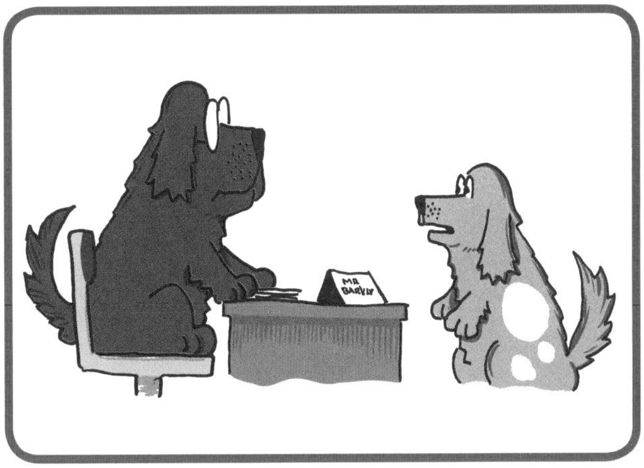
MR BARKLY

COMIC CREATOR

Use these blank panels to keep practicing your comic works of art!

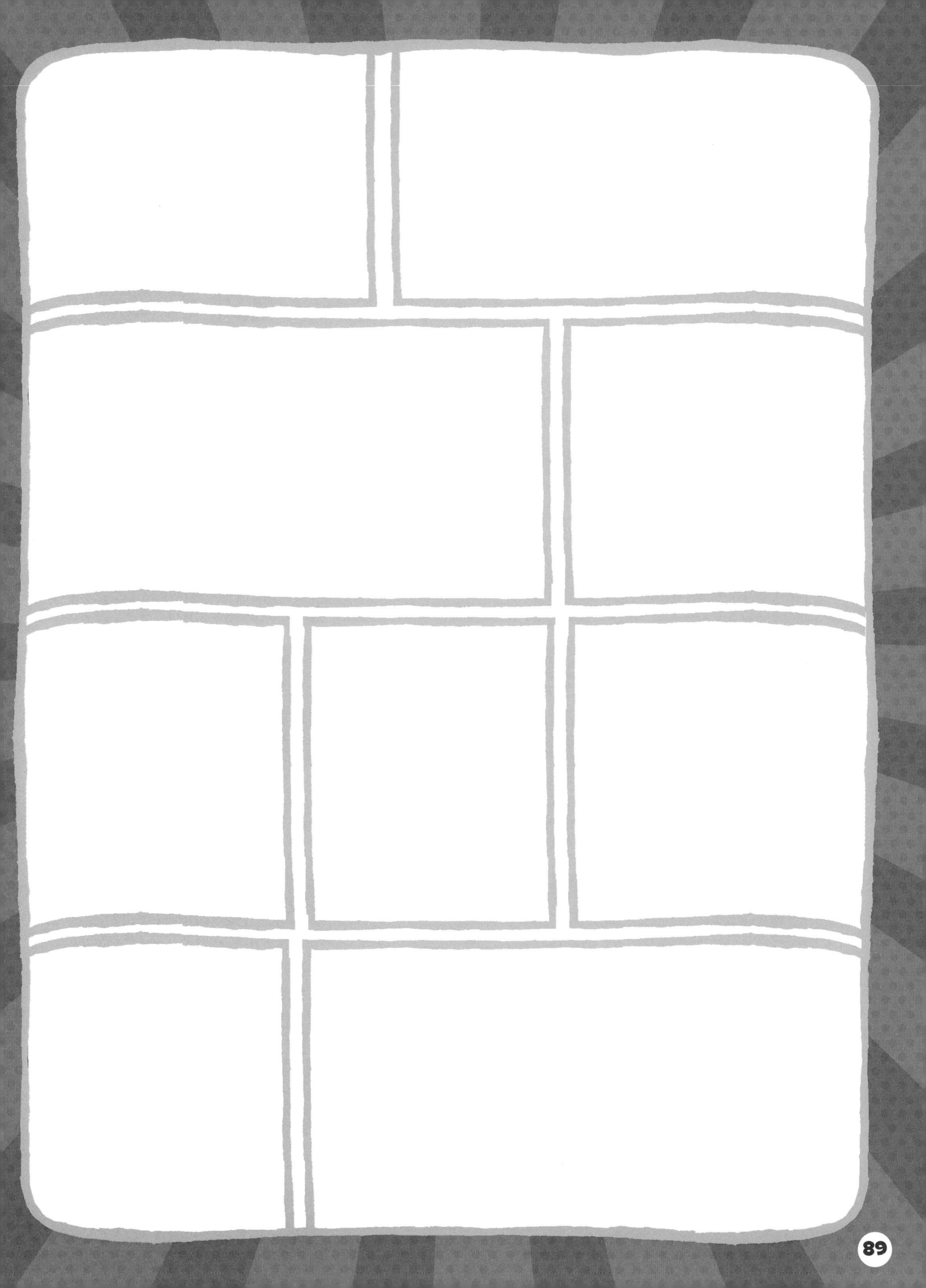

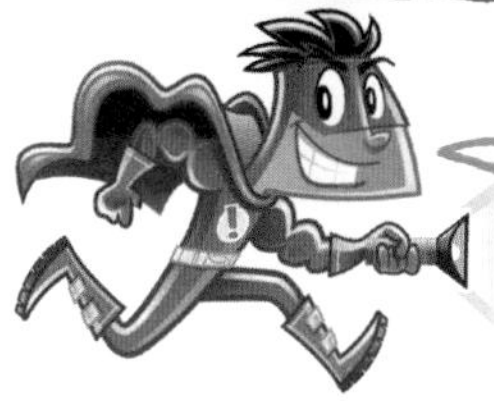

ANSWERS

Pages 6–7

1. Honey, I'm home!
2. I could hear you much better if you just texted me.
3. Do you swear to tell the *hole* truth?
4. Do you want to go *fishing*?
5. We knew it was your birthday, so we got you a little something!
6. We'll both have the *fly special*.
7. Too late.
8. Did you two get anything at the *flea* market?

Page 12

What do monsters go to water ski?
LAKE EERIE

What do you call a giant mummy?
GAUZILLA

What is a ghost's favorite party game?
HIDE-AND-GO-SHRIEK

What do monsters put on for sunny days?
SUNSCREAM

What is a ghost's favorite day?
FRIGHTDAY

Page 14

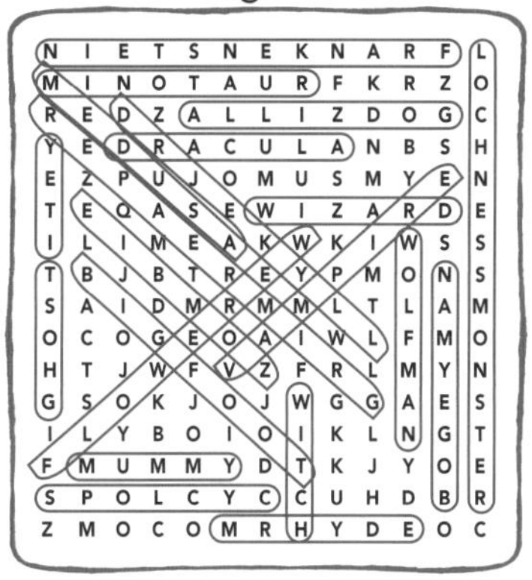

Page 15

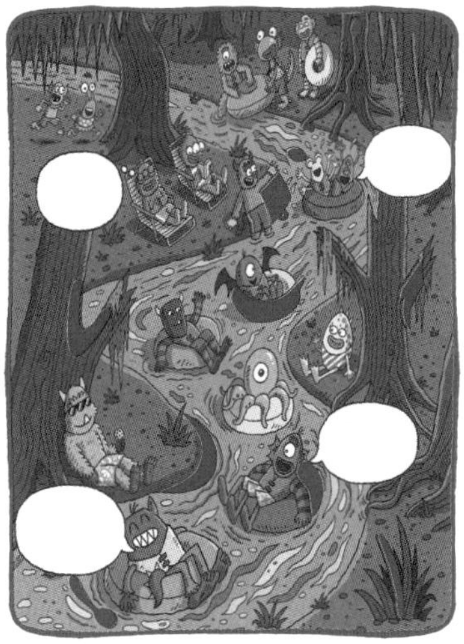

Pages 18–19

1. But if I sleep upside down, my phone will fall out of my pocket!
2. Waiter, there's a *hare* in my soup.
3. Well, how was I supposed to know you'd be flying a kite right here?
4. Do you have something *more* formal?
5. Nice try, but no cats allowed.
6. This is nothing. You should see what I can do to a *pencil*.
7. I'll *never* understand how humans do that.
8. Good news! No cavities. But I can't do anything about your *dog breath*.

Page 24

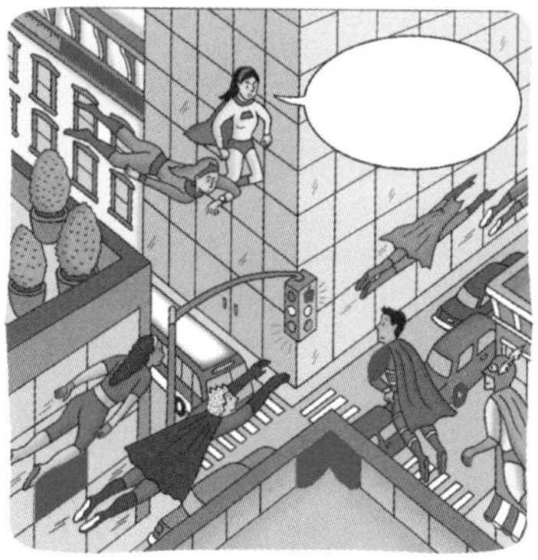

Page 28

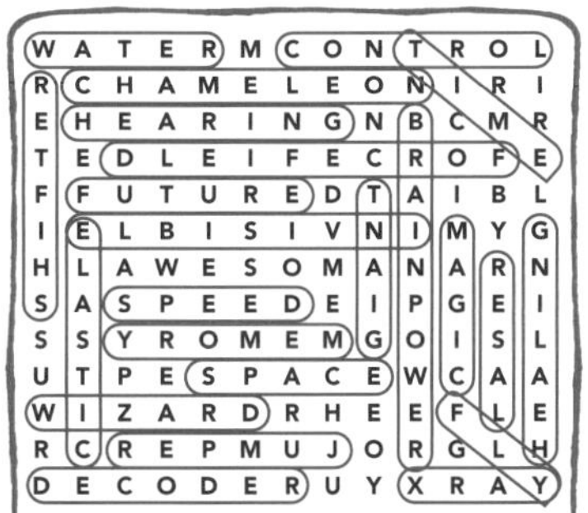

His name is MR. INCREDIBLY AWESOME SUPERHERO GUY!

Page 29

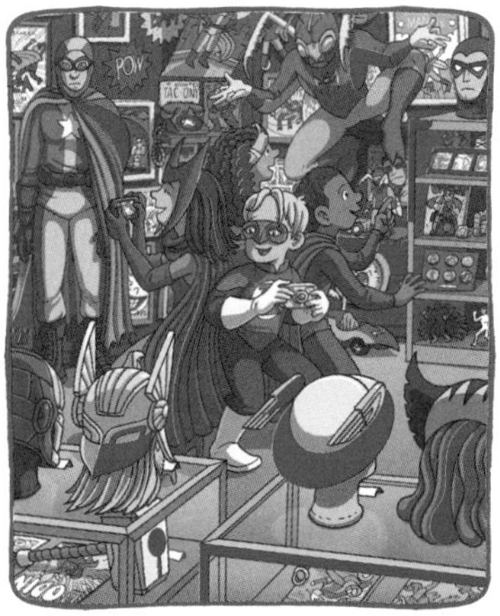

Pages 32–33

1. I *told* you not to stay in the sun too long!
2. I ate my homework.
3. Don't worry. No one's gonna care what you said 65 million years from now!
4. So . . . I guess you're not much for conversation?
5. Now *this* could be a game changer!
6. It's genuine Persian cat hair.
7. You'll *never* guess what I had for dinner.
8. Actually, it's for my dog.

ANSWERS

Page 38

Which birds are sad?
BLUE JAYS

What can turkeys use to play an instrument?
DRUMSTICKS

What do you give a sick bird?
TWEETMENT

What are smarter than talking birds?
SPELLING BEES

What do you get when you cross centipedes with parrots?
WALKIE-TALKIES

Page 40

1. JOEY
2. POULT
3. KIT
4. EYAS
5. CYGNET
6. CRIA
BONUS: "I'm just KITTEN!"

Page 41

Pages 44–45

1. Maybe if I keep digging, I'll find even *more* dirt!
2. Stop bulldozing? Okay, boss, if you're sure!
3. He has a point.
4. I *knew* this would work better with scarves!
5. I'm ready for Halloween.
6. The rabbit said to tell you that he quit.
7. I'm looking for something a bit more *permanent*.
8. Okay, I think this is high enough!

Page 50

Page 52

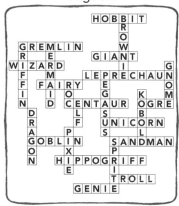

HOBBIT
BROWNIE
GREMLIN
GRIFFIN
MERMAID
GIANT
WIZARD
GNOME
LEPRECHAUN
FAIRY
ROC
PEGASUS
ELF
CENTAUR
KOBOLD
OGRE
DRAGON
UNICORN
PIXIE
GOBLIN
SANDMAN
HIPPOGRIFF
SPRITE
TROLL
GENIE

Page 53

LOOK AT THESE FOOTPRINTS! THEY'RE THREE TIMES THE SIZE OF MINE!
WE BETTER FOLLOW THEM!
LOOK, THAT MUST BE BIGFOOT!
ARE YOU BIGFOOT?
NO, I'M JUST BORROWING HIS SHOES.

Pages 56–57

1. Excuse me, which way to the pool?
2. *Odor* in the court!
3. Thanks! Now I can figure out how old I am!
4. Sorry, that's as high as I can push you!
5. Happy birthday to *ewe*!
6. *Riiiiiiing*! Not so much fun, is it?
7. Sure, it's easy for *you*!
8. I'm sorry. I have 99 left feet.

ANSWERS

Pages 58–59

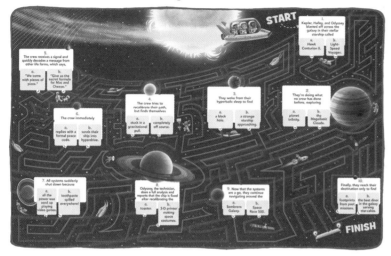

START
FINISH

Page 62

START
FINISH

Page 63

Page 66

INTERSTELLAR ELEMENTARY

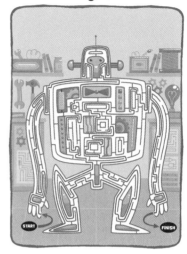

Page 67

How did the rocket lose its job?
IT GOT FIRED.

What meals do astronauts like best?
LAUNCH

What do young astronauts like to read?
COMET BOOKS

Pages 70–71

1. I *love* your goatee!
2. Take me to your discount shoe store.
3. Do you have this one in extra *wide*?
4. We're going on a hike. See you later!
5. It's time to do your chores, Gregory! Please go take *in* the trash!
6. Okay, who circled all this *stuff* in the pet store catalog?!
7. Row, row, row your *goat* . . .
8. Hey, man! Gimme *two*!

Pages 76–77

Here are some rhymes we found. You may have found others.

bat hat	fly pie	owl towel
bear pear	fox box	parrot carrot
bee key	frog log	red sled
big pig	gator waiter	sand hand
book hook	ghost toast	seal wheel
brown gown	green bean	sheep sweep
cone phone	hill drill	snail sail
corn horn	king sing	tree ski
crow bow	lake snake	whale scale
double bubble	moose juice	wide slide

ANSWERS

Pages 78–79

WANTED
YUL B. SORRY
WANTED
MR. REE
WANTED
BEN DONNE
WANTED
LOUIS TOOTH
WANTED
ALENE MACHINE
WANTED
CONSTANCE BICKERING
WANTED
AVA LANCH
WANTED
DELIA CARDS
WANTED
HARRY FACE
WANTED
KENT STOP

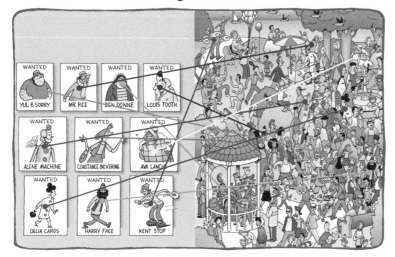

Page 80

Page 84

1. POP
2. OUCH
3. GROWL
4. GLUG
5. RING
6. VROOM
7. SIZZLE
8. POOF
9. PURR
10. CHIRP
11. ACHOO
12. BUZZ

Published by Highlights Press
815 Church Street
Honesdale, Pennsylvania 18431
ISBN: 978-1-62979-949-0
Manufactured in Dongguan, Guangdong, China
Mfg. 10/2023

First edition
Visit our website at Highlights.com.
10 9 8 7 6 5 4 3 2 1

Cut out the sticker sheet here.

9949S-01

PAGES 6–7 THE COMIC PAGES

DID YOU TWO GET ANYTHING AT THE ***FLEA*** MARKET?

I COULD HEAR YOU MUCH BETTER IF YOU JUST TEXTED ME.

HONEY, I'M HOME!

DO YOU WANT TO GO ***FISHING***?

DO YOU SWEAR TO TELL THE ***HOLE*** TRUTH?

TOO LATE.

WE KNEW IT WAS YOUR BIRTHDAY, SO WE GOT YOU A LITTLE SOMETHING!

WE'LL BOTH HAVE THE ***FLY SPECIAL***.

9949S-01

PAGES 18–19 THE COMIC PAGES

GOOD NEWS! NO CAVITIES. BUT I CAN'T DO ANYTHING ABOUT YOUR ***DOG BREATH***.

THIS IS NOTHING. YOU SHOULD SEE WHAT I CAN DO TO A ***PENCIL***!

WELL, HOW WAS I SUPPOSED TO KNOW YOU'D BE FLYING A KITE RIGHT HERE?

NICE TRY, BUT NO CATS ALLOWED.

DO YOU HAVE SOMETHING ***MORE*** FORMAL?

WAITER, THERE'S A ***HARE*** IN MY SOUP.

BUT IF I SLEEP UPSIDE DOWN, MY PHONE WILL FALL OUT OF MY POCKET!

I'LL ***NEVER*** UNDERSTAND HOW HUMANS DO THAT.

PAGES 32–33 THE COMIC PAGES

YOU'LL ***NEVER*** GUESS WHAT I HAD FOR DINNER.

NOW ***THIS*** COULD BE A GAME CHANGER!

SO . . . I GUESS YOU'RE NOT MUCH FOR CONVERSATION?

I ATE MY HOMEWORK.

IT'S GENUINE PERSIAN CAT HAIR.

ACTUALLY, IT'S FOR MY DOG.

DON'T WORRY. NO ONE'S GONNA CARE WHAT YOU SAID 65 MILLION YEARS FROM NOW!

I ***TOLD*** YOU NOT TO STAY IN THE SUN TOO LONG!

9949S-01

Cut out the sticker sheet here.

PAGES 44–45 THE COMIC PAGES

I'M LOOKING FOR SOMETHING A BIT MORE ***PERMANENT***.

MAYBE IF I KEEP DIGGING, I'LL FIND EVEN ***MORE*** DIRT!

THE RABBIT SAID TO TELL YOU THAT HE QUIT.

HE HAS A POINT.

STOP BULLDOZING? OKAY, BOSS, IF YOU'RE SURE!

I'M READY FOR HALLOWEEN.

OKAY, I THINK THIS IS HIGH ENOUGH!

I ***KNEW*** THIS WOULD WORK BETTER WITH SCARVES!

9949S-01

PAGES 56–57 THE COMIC PAGES

I'M SORRY. I HAVE 99 LEFT FEET.

EXCUSE ME, WHICH WAY TO THE POOL?

RIIIIIIING! NOT SO MUCH FUN, IS IT?

SORRY, THAT'S AS HIGH AS I CAN PUSH YOU!

THANKS! NOW I CAN FIGURE OUT HOW OLD I AM!

ODOR IN THE COURT!

HAPPY BIRTHDAY TO ***EWE***!

SURE, IT'S EASY FOR ***YOU***!

9949S-01

PAGES 70–71 THE COMIC PAGES

TAKE ME TO YOUR DISCOUNT SHOE STORE.

ROW, ROW, ROW YOUR ***GOAT***...

IT'S TIME TO DO YOUR CHORES, GREGORY! PLEASE GO TAKE ***IN*** THE TRASH!

HEY, MAN! GIMME ***TWO***!

WE'RE GOING ON A HIKE. SEE YOU LATER!

OKAY, WHO CIRCLED ALL THIS ***STUFF*** IN THE PET STORE CATALOG?!

DO YOU HAVE THIS ONE IN EXTRA ***WIDE***?

I ***LOVE*** YOUR GOATEE!

9949S-01

Cut out the sticker sheet here.

9949S-01

PAGES 10–11 MONSTER DOODLES

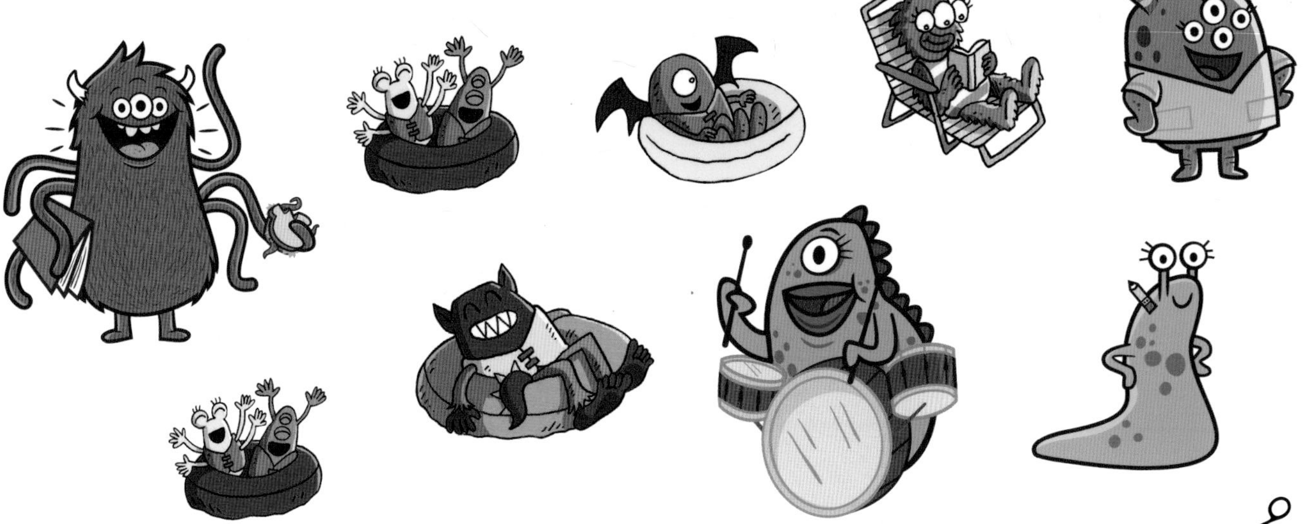

PAGES 26–27 SUPERHERO DOODLES

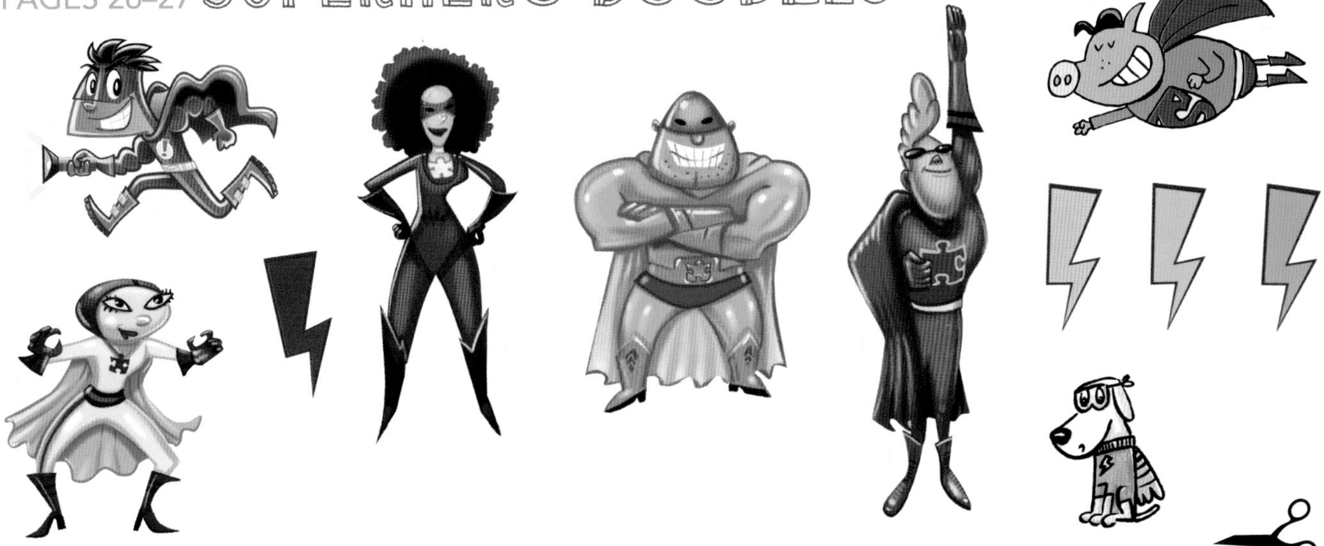

9949S-01

PAGES 36–37 ANIMAL DOODLES

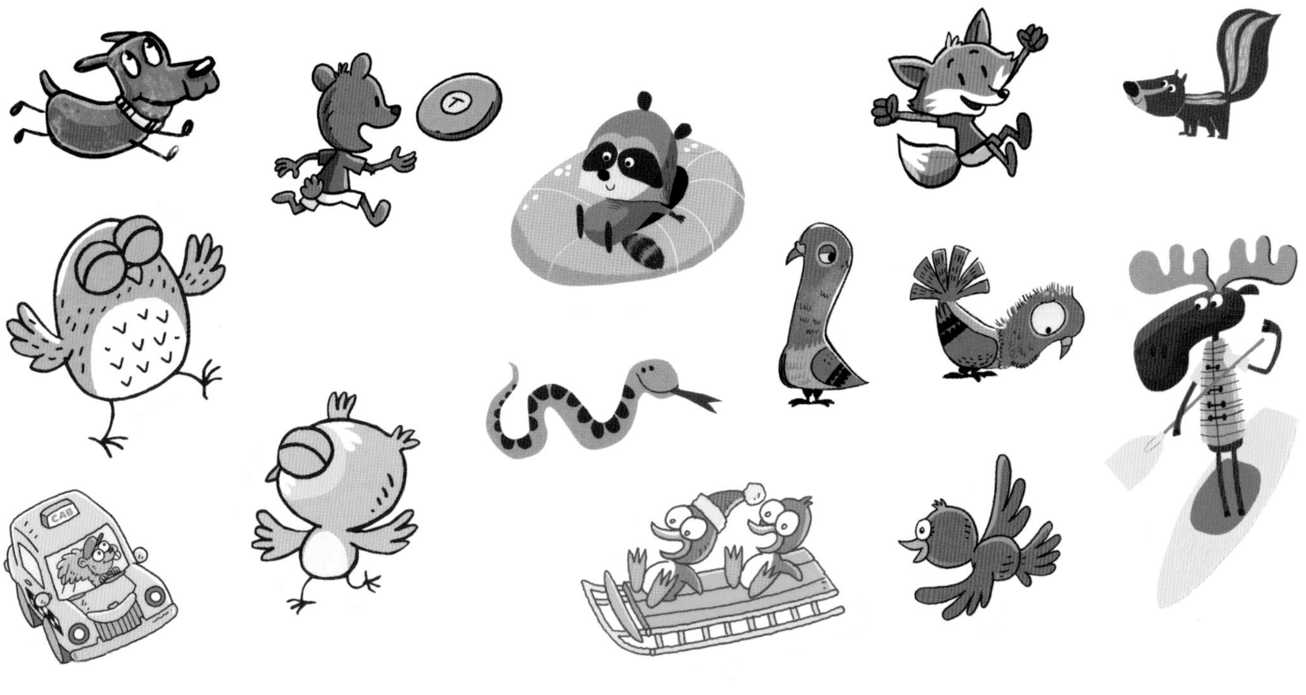
CAB

9949S-01

Cut out the sticker sheet here.

9949S-01

PAGES 48–49 MYTHICAL DOODLES

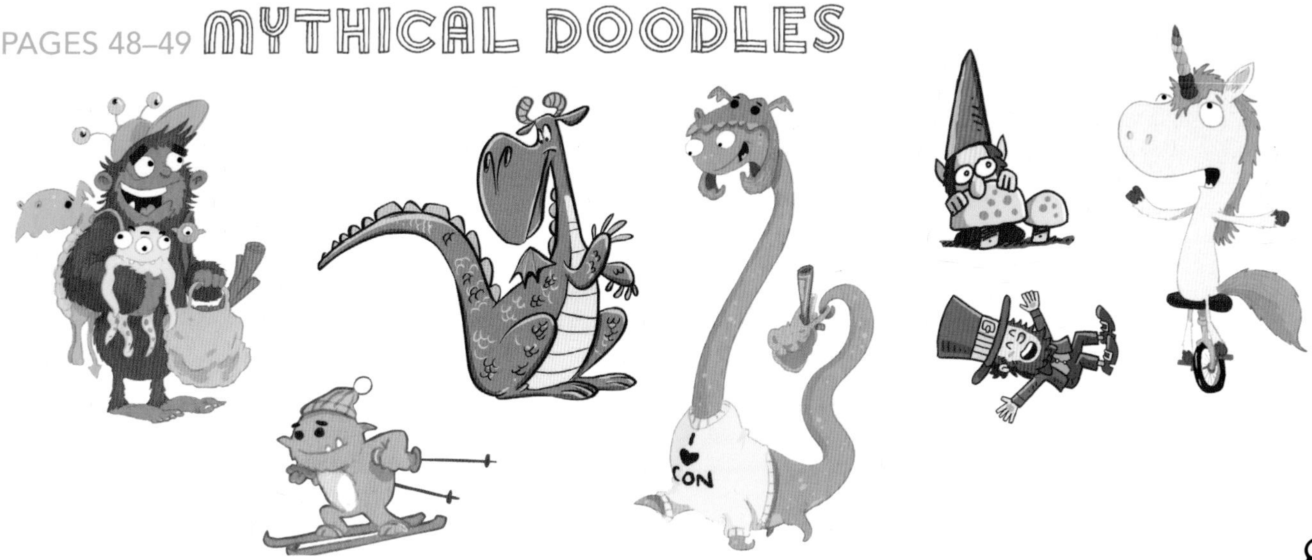
I
CON

9949S-01

PAGES 60–61 SPACE DOODLES

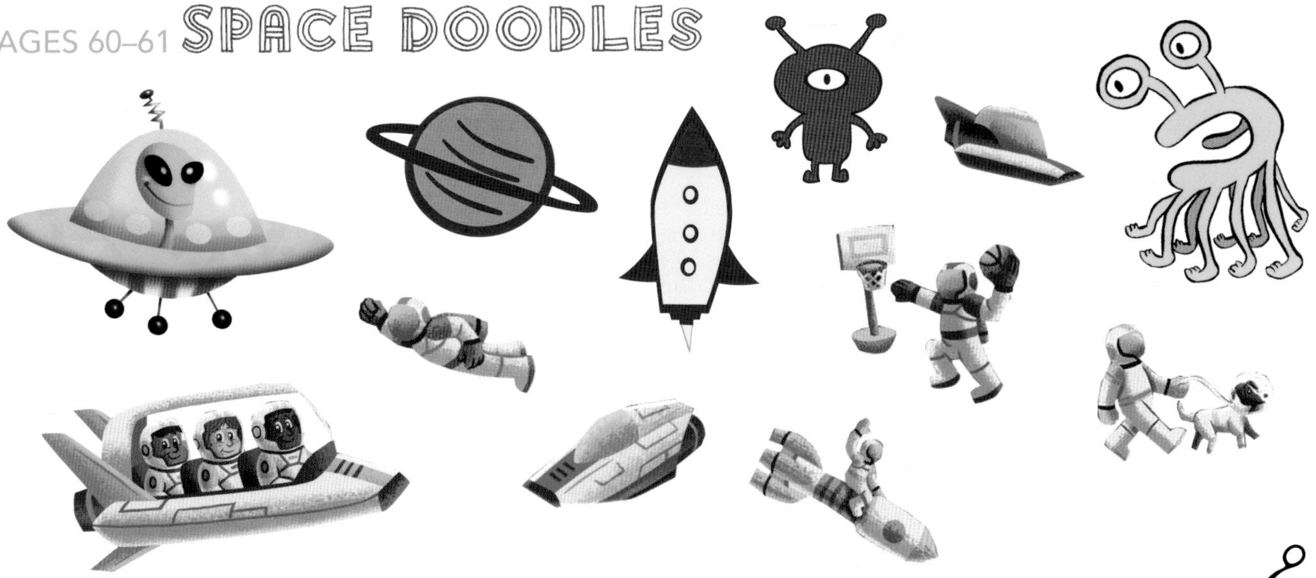

9949S-01

PAGES 76–77 SCENE OF THE RHYME

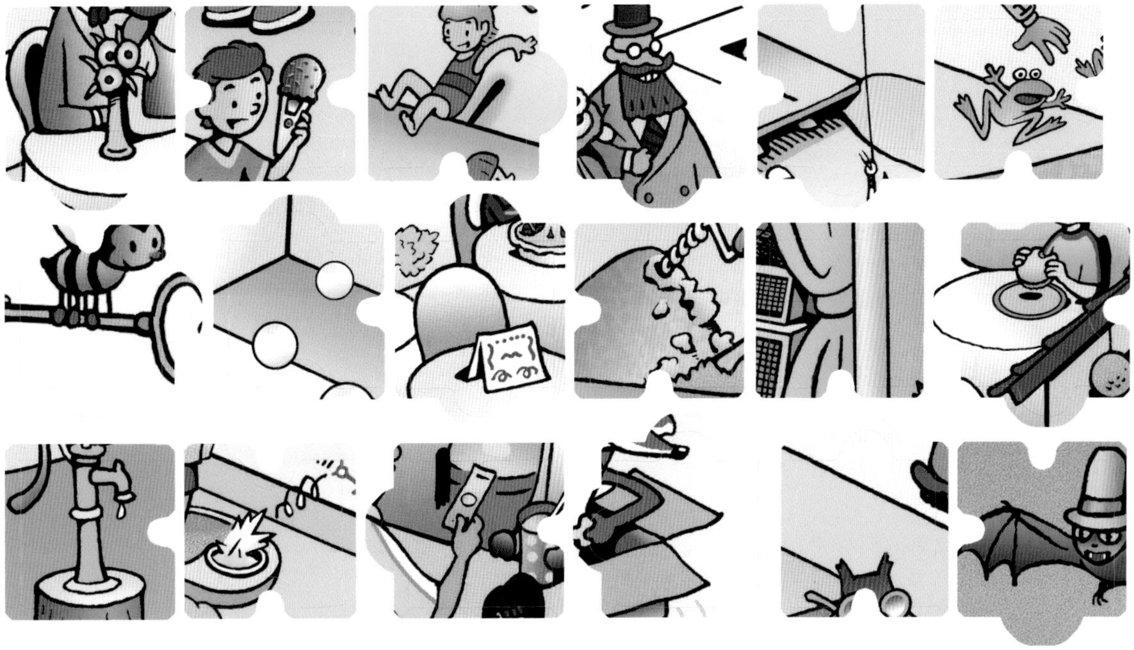

Cut out the sticker sheet here.

PAGES 74–75 DETECTIVE DOODLES

CRIME SCENE DO NOT CROSS

CRIME SCENE DO NOT CROSS

9949S-01

PAGES 22–23 STICKER SOUND EFFECTS

BOOM
ZAP!
POOF
POW
WHAM!
OOPS!
BANG!
SPLASH!
POW
POOF

9949S-01

PAGE 13 STICKER STORY

MIXTAPES	INTERIOR DECORATORS	WITCHES	BOGEYMEN
MASCOTS	HEALTH INSPECTORS	GHOSTS	MUMMIES
BOOKSTORES	CHOCOLATE FACTORIES	ZOMBIES	NIGHT CLASSES
LOVE LETTERS	GOBLINS	VAMPIRES	BROOM CLOSETS

9949S-01

Cut out the sticker sheet here.

PAGE 65 **BUILD A BOT**

YOU'RE MY MOST RUSTED FRIEND.

WOULD YOU LIKE TO HEAR A JOKE?

STOP PUSHING MY BUTTONS.

BEEP BOOP BEEP BOOP

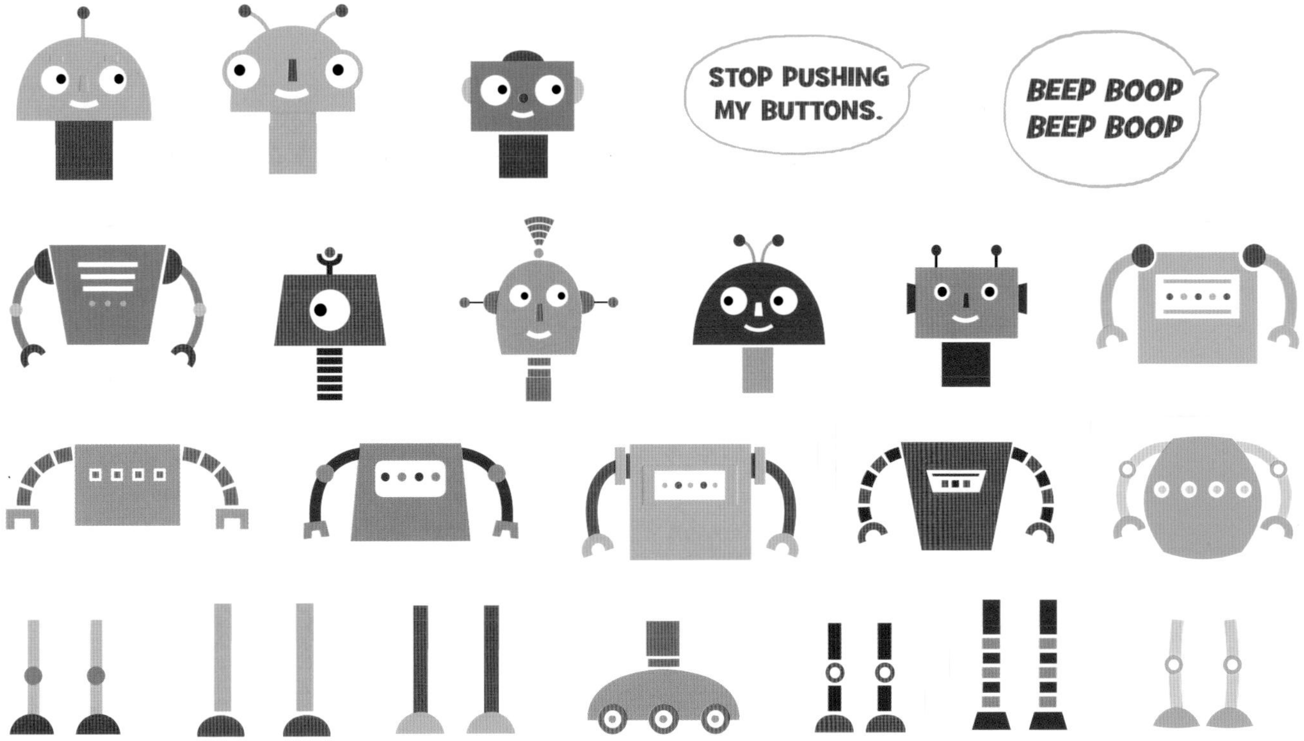

BONUS STICKERS

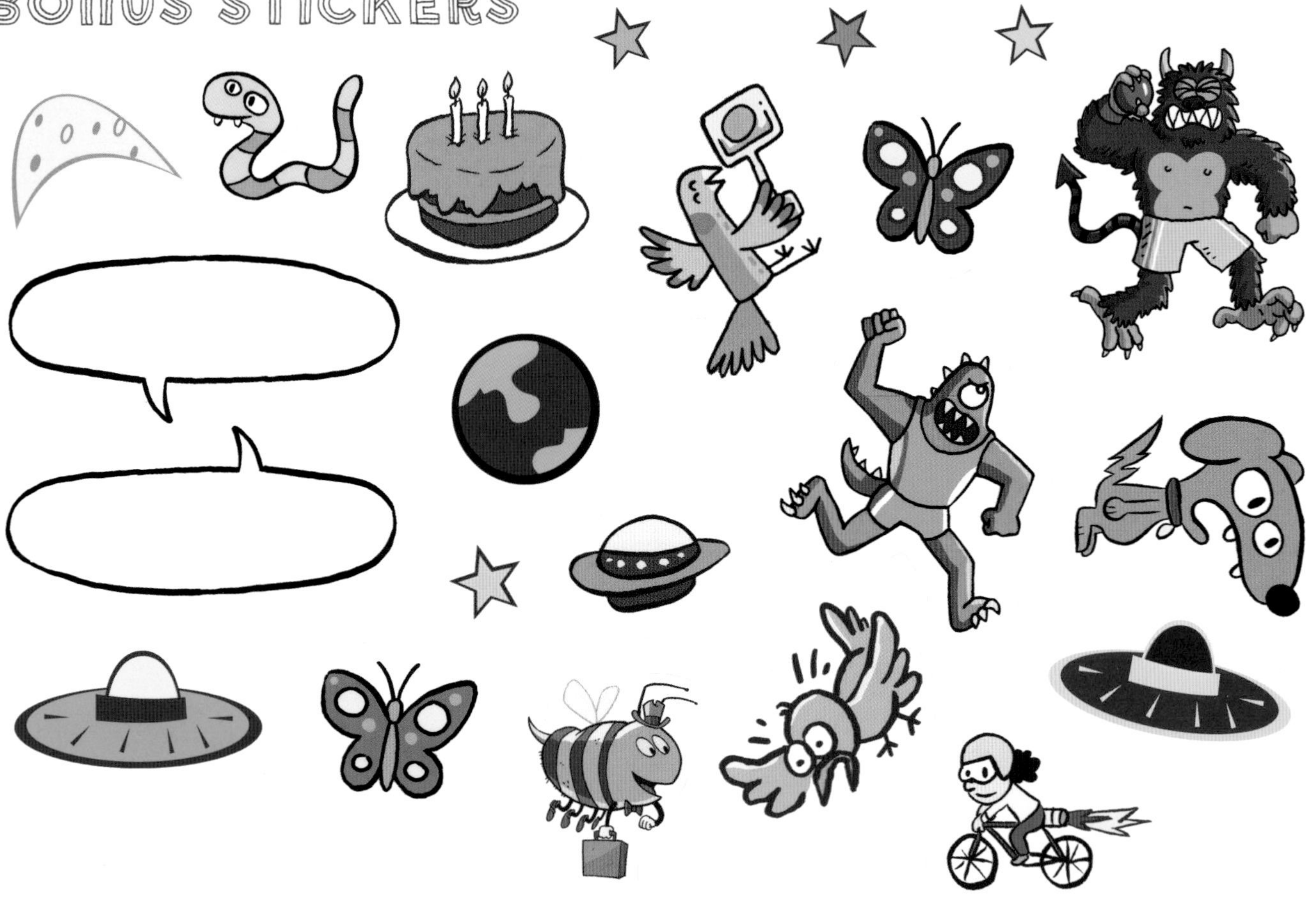

9949S-01

9949S-01